SIMPLY BRUSCHETTA
garlic toast the italian way

SIMPLY BRUSCHETTA

garlic toast the italian way

vittorio pellegrino

Maui arThoughts Company
P.O. Box 967
Wailuku, HI, USA 96793-0967
Phone/Fax: 808-244-0156
Phone/Fax Toll Free (orders): 800-403-3472
E-mail: books@maui.net
Websites: booksmaui.com OR mauiarthoughts.com

Pellegrino, Vittorio Carlo
SIMPLY BRUSCHETTA—Garlic Toast the Italian Way
International Standard Book Number: 0-945045-06-9
Library of Congress Card Number: 00-192133

Food Images courtesy of Hemera Technologies, Inc.
Food Photography by Vittorio Pellegrino
Cover Design by Vittorio Pellegrino
Printed in the Republic of Korea

Published by: Maui arThoughts Company
            P.O. Box 967
            Wailuku, HI, USA 96793-0967
            Phone/Fax: 808-244-0156
            Phone/Fax Toll Free (orders): 800-403-3472
            E-mail: books@maui.net
            Websites: booksmaui.com OR mauiarthoughts.com

Publisher's Cataloging-in-Publication
(Provided by Quality Books, Inc.)

Pellegrino, Victor C.
    Simply bruschetta : garlic toast the Italian way /
Vittorio Pellegrino. -- 1st ed.
     p. cm.
     Includes index.
     ISBN: 0-945045-06-9

     1. Sandwiches. 2. Cookery (Bread) 3. Cookery,
Italian.   I. Title

TX818.P45 2001   641.8'15
            QBI00-714

DEDICATION

To my wife

Wallette Pualani Lyn-fah

To my children

Shelley Jeanne La'ela'eokalā Lyn-oi

Angela Terese Mahinamalamalama Mei-lyn

Hōkūao Christopher Joseph Bailey Wu-wei

To my parents

Albert and Adeline Pellegrino

ACKNOWLEDGMENTS

I wish to acknowledge my Italian family and ancestors,
who in many ways have had much to do
with who I am and the creation of

SIMPLY BRUSCHETTA

garlic toast the italian way

Grazie,
Vittorio Pellegrino

Madalina Pellegrino
Angelo Pellegrino
Maria DiDomenico Pellegrino
Albert Pellegrino
Valentino Pellegrino
Louis Pellegrino
Madeline Pellegrino
Margaret Pellegrino
Mary Pellegrino
Angelina Pellegrino
Victor Pellegrino I
Theresa Pellegrino
Alfred Pellegrino

Carlo Falcone
Maria DiPonziano Falcone
Adeline Falcone
Assunta Falcone
Americo Falcone
Dominic Falcone I
Dominic Falcone II
Angeline Falcone
Leonard Falcone
James Falcone
Anna Falcone

"I am you, you are me, and we are one."
Pellegrino, V., Maui Art Thoughts—Expressions and Visions © 1988

CONTENTS

Introduction   11
Two Steps to Preparing Bruschetta Con Aglio   15
    Preparing the Toast   15
    Preparing and Applying the Garlic and Olive Oil   15
Measurements, Proportions, and Servings   17
Italian Cheese   18
The Cardinal Rules for Italian Cheese   19
Bread   20
Olive Oil   22
Garlic   23
Variations, Substitutions and Repetition   24
Bruschetta Recipes   25
    Traditional Bruschetta Con Aglio   27
    Pesto   28
    Pepper Rainbow   29
    Broccoli Rabc   30
    Oregano, Tomato and Onion   31
    Anchovy   32
    Gorgonzola and Red Onion   33
    Anise   34
    Marinara Sauce   35
    Sun-Dried Tomato   36
    Roma Plum Tomato and Basil   37
    Red Chili Pepper   38
    Italian Sausage, Peppers and Onions   39
    Portabella Mushroom   40
    Roasted Garlic   41
    Prosciutto and Melon   42
    Mixed Greens   43
    Salmon and Capers   44
    Pine Nuts, Currants and Tomato   45
    Roasted Peppers   46
    Tomato and Oregano   47
    Zucchini   48
    Orange and Anchovy   49
    Grilled Tomato   50
    Sweet Caribe Banana Pepper   51

Ricotta and Olive   52
Artichoke, Roasted Pepper and Plum Tomato   53
Baked Eggplant   54
Rosemary, Red Onion and Chili Pepper   55
Dandelion Greens and Bacon   56
Grilled Eggplant and Mozzarella   57
Cucumber and Balsamic Vinegar   58
Artichoke   59
Shallots and Tomato   60
Olive   61
Chicken Liver Pâte'   62
Spinach and Egg   63
Fried Polenta Sans Toast   64
Three Peppercorns   65
Egg and Cheese   66
Marinated Eggplant   67
Green Tomato   68
Asparagus   69
Fava   70
Fried Onions and Green Peppers   71
Bone Marrow   72
Sardines and Lemon   73
Drowned Bruschetta   74
Fried Cardoon   75
Tomato, Anchovy and Scallions   76
Broccolini   77
Finocchio and Pimiento   78
Beans and Greens   79
Fried Mozzarella   80
Roma Plum Tomato Rub   81
Chestnut   82
Caponata   83
Arugula and Plum Tomato   84
Butternut Squash, Pine Nuts and Bacon   85
Grilled Vegetables   86
Artichoke, Olive and Tomato   87
Shredded Chicken   88
Fried Garlic   89
Eggplant Spread   90
Salmon, Tomato and Onion   91
Finale'   92
Index   93
About the Author   94

INTRODUCTION

Bruschetta con aglio, pronounced brus-ketta′ con a′lyo (pronounce the *u* as in *you*, the *ch* as *k*, and the *e* as in *bet*), translates as toast with garlic. It originated in the northwestern province of Tuscany, where it is called *fettunata*, or "oiled slice." Many view *fettunata* as the perfect marriage of garlic, olive oil, and coarse salt on toasted bread. Waverley Root, author of *The Food of Italy*, notes that the Romans called the oiled garlic toast *bruschetto*, but that other Italians referred to it as *schiena d'asino*, or ass's back. Regardless of history, *bruschetta con aglio* is a favorite appetizer among Italians, both at home and in restaurants. Italians have taken the basic *bruschetta con aglio* and added foods to the top. Once a food topping or combination of food toppings is put on the toast, it is simply referred to as *bruschetta*.

Bruschetta can be served as a traditional *antipasto* or it can serve as a meal in itself accompanied by a wedge of sharp Italian cheese, a crisp garden salad, a cluster of grapes, and a bottle of full-bodied red wine. Either way, your family, guests, or restaurant patrons will find *bruschetta* a joy to the palate.

Bruschetta has always been one of my favorite Italian foods. It took little effort for the tastes, textures, and visual experiences to convince and motivate me to share my joy and enthusiasm with others. Thus, *SIMPLY BRUSCHETTA—Garlic Toast the Italian Way* was born. The main purpose of this book is to provide a wide variety of toppings, sixty-five in all, for those like me who have nearly an addiction to this wonderful Italian *antipasto*. And once you begin preparing your own *bruschetta*, it is sure to become one of your favorite foods, too.

Americans are catching on to *bruschetta* almost as fast as they have adopted pizza and pasta. In some of America's larger cities, it is served as an individual appetizer or part of the antipasti. In all likelihood, its popularity is increasing because it combines two key interests among Americans who prepare meals at home: it is very tasty and most recipes are quick and easy to prepare. In addition, one need not seek out the "Italian section" of town, for many once-hard-to-get ingredients are readily available in local supermarkets.

Preparing *bruschetta con aglio* is a very simple process. There are four basic steps: 1) toasting both sides of thick slices of a rustic Italian bread (grilling over charcoal is the original and still the best method); 2) rubbing fresh garlic around the top edges of the crust and onto the entire surface while still hot—using the bread as a kind of "sandpaper;" 3) lightly drizzling a fruity, extra virgin olive oil on top; and 4) sprinkling the toast with sea salt. More and more, cooks are adding freshly ground black peppercorns. As a note of warning, however, remember that Italians do not use butter as a substitute for olive oil. Although butter is a rather standard but unauthentic substitute used by Americans, Italians visiting here would find it unacceptable—to put it mildly.

Today, both chefs and home cooks are adding a new dimension to *bruschetta con aglio* by combining it with the toppings familiar to Italian *crostino (kro-ste′-no),* or canape′. In my view, it is a perfect marriage, and adding traditional or newly created toppings does not make preparation complex or overly time consuming.

To me, the joy to making *bruschetta* lies in its toppings and spreads. You can engage in being authentically Italian, or you can create a topping or combination topping according to whim or using serious planning and creativity. As long as you begin with the same basics and original approach that I describe in *SIMPLY BRUSCHETTA—Garlic Toast the Italian Way*, there is no limit to the kinds of unique toppings that you can make to create tasty and unique *bruschetta*.

Note that most of my recipes focus mainly on vegetables. Only a few recipes contain fish (anchovy, salmon, and sardines), fowl (chicken, chicken liver), or meat (prosciutto, pancetta, bacon, beef bone marrow, ham hock, and Italian sausage). Although you can experiment with other ingredients, I recommend, favor, and enjoy vegetables for *bruschetta*. Vegetables were common in our Italian household and, more often than not, they made up the better part of the Italian dishes we prepared; so it is not surprising that my recipes reflect that fact. Last of all, more vegetables and less meat in one's diet is a healthier way to eat.

There are a few important comments about preparing *bruschetta* that cannot be left unsaid. As in all of my recipes, simplicity of preparation comes first. Of course, taste is the most important element, and the variety of tastes one can produce with *bruschetta* make it simultaneously versatile and elegant. Visually, food should delight the eye and excite the palate. *Bruschetta* fulfills all of these criteria, but most of all, each topping for *bruschetta* produces a surprise—to the delight of the cook and to those who join in what can be an appetizer or a feast!

Last of all, a note about my philosophy of cooking. The aim of all of my recipes and cooking encourages one to experiment, to invent, and to create. You should be no different in the kitchen than a composer at the piano, a dancer on the stage, or an artist in a studio. After all, food *is* art. We listen to it sizzle, we move about the kitchen as in a dance, and we serve food, glistening in a variety of colors and shapes. But the best part of the art of cooking goes beyond music, dance and painting: we can consume our "food art" to nourish our bodies and to elevate our spirits.

Try all sixty-five *bruschetta* recipes in SIMPLY BRUSCHETTA—*Garlic Toast the Italian Way*. Feel free to experiment by adding, deleting, or modifying ingredients in a recipe to meet your tastes and your guests' preferences. For example, you can reduce or increase the amount of garlic, use a bread different than Italian, or try toppings unique to your own geographical region, seasons, or national origin. Last of all, try the finale´ at the end of the book for one of your dinner parties.

Should you discover any unique toppings or have any suggestions for new combinations of toppings, take a few minutes and mail them to Vittorio Pellegrino, *SIMPLY BRUSCHETTA—Garlic Toast the Italian Way*, P.O. Box 967, Wailuku, HI, USA 96793-0967; fax them to 1-808-244-0156; or you can e-mail them to books@maui.net

P.S. Each of my recipes is preceded by one of my aphorisms. Some of these aphorisms are new, having been written specifically for this cookbook. Others have been taken, as is or revised, from my book of sayings, published in 1988, titled *Maui Art Thoughts—Expressions and Visions*. Think about each aphorism as you enjoy preparing and eating your own *bruschetta*.

Buon appetito!
Vittorio Pellegrino
Waikapu, Maui, Hawai'i
2001

BRUSCHETTA

Two Steps to Preparing Bruschetta Con Aglio

Preparing the Toast

Preparing and Applying the Garlic and Olive Oil

Measurements, Proportions, and Servings

Italian Cheese

The Cardinal Rules for Italian Cheese

Bread

Olive Oil

Garlic

Variations, Substitutions and Repetition

TWO STEPS TO PREPARING BRUSCHETTA CON AGLIO

1) PREPARING THE TOAST

The traditional and best method of preparing Italian bread toast is grilling both sides (about a minute or two) over charcoal. This melds a unique smoky flavor with the uneven browning design to create artistry in each slice.

Start with a loaf of unsliced Italian bread. As a matter of preference, Italians like their bread to be two or three days old; as a result, the toast accepts the garlic better because of its crustier surface. Stale bread is also used. If a good Italian bread is unavailable, you can bake your own. French bread is a good substitute, too. See *Bread*, page 20.

Cut eight thick slices of bread. One inch is a good thickness. I prefer to cut my bread diagonally to create larger slices. If you cannot charcoal grill your bread, arrange the slices on a baking sheet and broil them in an oven, about six inches from the heating element. Broil each side until golden brown—about two minutes for each side. (Distance from the heating element and the amount of time to broil the bread will differ according to your oven. Watch the bread closely to avoid burning.) Besides charcoal or oven broiling, several different approaches to toasting the slices of bread will produce excellent results: a toaster oven, a counter top oven broiler or a wide slice toaster.

Last of all, garlic must be applied to one side of the toast (top) while it is still hot, followed by drizzling on extra virgin olive oil and by sprinkling on coarse sea salt to taste.

2) PREPARING AND APPLYING THE GARLIC AND OLIVE OIL

Like a composer, I like to prepare foods based on a theme and variation. Thus, I frequently substitute one spice or food for another—say hot, red chili pepper for black peppercorns, or Parmigiano-Reggiano for Pecorino Romano.

But when it comes to choosing garlic, I find there is no perfect substitute for a fresh bulb, and when it comes to choosing olive oil for *bruschetta con aglio*, extra virgin olive oil has no equal. These are what Italians use, but that is not the only reason. The fact is, fresh garlic has a unique texture, flavor and chemistry that prepared or processed garlic does not possess, and extra virgin olive oil has a taste, color, and aroma that is unequaled.

Once slices of Italian bread have been grilled, toasted, or broiled (both sides), use one of the two methods outlined below for the best tasting *bruschetta con aglio*. The first method is the traditional way; the second is a good substitute.

1) Peel one or two cloves of garlic (uncrushed). Use them whole. Rub the garlic back and forth and all around the top edges of the crust and onto the entire surface of each slice of toasted Italian bread (top side only and while the bread is hot). Then either drizzle extra virgin olive oil onto each slice, or using a pastry brush, coat the top edges of the crust and the entire surface of each slice, again while the bread is still hot. Use one third to one half cup of extra virgin olive oil for eight large slices.

2) Using a large knife, crush one or two cloves of garlic with the flat side of the blade. Remove the skin. Using a mortar and pestle, blend and mash the garlic until it is smooth and pasty. Add one third to one half cup of extra virgin olive oil and blend well. With a pastry brush, spread the mixture all around the top edges of the crust and onto the entire surface of each slice of toasted Italian bread while it is still hot.

Note: For each of the two methods, the number of cloves of garlic and the amount of extra virgin olive oil may be altered—that is reduced or increased—based on the size of the slices of bread as well as on personal preference.

MEASUREMENTS
PROPORTIONS AND SERVINGS

Following recipes with total exactness is not always possible, and creating recipes with strict rigidity is sometimes unrealistic. Sometimes recipes require a cook's creativity, and at other times, sizes or proportions may vary, thus requiring altering the menu. Therefore, there are two important reminders I wish to make clear to my readers concerning measurements and proportions for *bruschetta*.

1) Because the shapes (long, round, etc...) and sizes (diameter or circumference) of Italian bread differ, not only among Italian bread makers but also bakers from other countries, you may have toppings left over or, in some circumstances, not enough. In some cases you may need more extra virgin olive oil or additional cloves of garlic; in other cases, less. Should this occur, solutions are simple. If you have too much, either make more slices of *bruschetta*, or save the toppings. Use the leftover oil and garlic for other recipes. Should you have too little, make smaller or fewer slices of *bruschetta*.

2) I purposely omitted the measurement for sea salt and black peppercorns in most recipes, particularly because the amount used is purely a matter of diet and health reasons, taste, personal preference, and sometimes a matter of taking into account the wishes of your family or guests.

3) For some recipes I have omitted salt. For example, *bruschetta* with anchovy, salmon and capers, and gorgonzola and red onion will be salty enough without adding sea salt.

4) You can sprinkle sea salt on *bruschetta* by hand, or you can use a mortar and pestle or a mill if you wish to make a finer grind.

5) After you follow the recipes for *bruschetta* several times, you will develop an eye and feel for amounts. You have only to remember asking your mom just how much of this or that was needed for a particular dish. She never could say, exactly, but her recipes always turned out perfectly. You will find the same true for yourself. If you are like me, you can make notes in your recipe books when you don't want to forget some modifications in the ingredients or procedures.

6) Finally, the number of servings for each recipe is eight, assuming one slice of *bruschetta* per person. The size of the loaf of Italian bread or another kind of bread will determine the number of slices needed per serving. For example, you might make sixteen slices if you were using a French baguette or an Italian sfilation (Italian baguette).

ITALIAN CHEESE

Nine different kinds of Italian cheeses are used in the variety of *bruschetta* recipes.

Asiago is made from partially skimmed cow's milk. It is a sharp, salty cheese that is excellent for grating and best used as a cooking ingredient rather than eaten by itself.

Fontina is made from unskimmed and unpasteurized cow's milk. This semisoft cheese possesses a delicate flavor. It is yellow in color, contains small holes, and has a very fat, creamy texture.

Fontinella is made from goat or cow's milk. It is a sharp cheese with a smooth texture, and it is an excellent choice for grilling or broiling. Do not confuse it with Fontina.

Gorgonzola is made from pasteurized cow's milk. This semisoft, creamy and crumbly cheese ranges from mild to sharp, the latter having a tangy "bite." Sometimes referred to as the Italian "blue" cheese, it is actually a pale yellow with grey-green marbled or veined mold. Gorgonzola is best eaten at room temperature.

Mozzarella is made from buffalo milk. It is a soft, smooth, unsalted white cheese. Compared to most Italian cheeses, it is bland and is best enhanced with spices or complemented by other foods.

Parmigiano-Reggiano is made from semi-skimmed unpasteurized cow's milk. It is a strong cheese, pale yellow in color, and makes an excellent grating cheese after it ages three to four years and becomes hard. It has a grainy, rough and crumbly texture and a nutty flavor. A lesser quality Parmesan cheese is Grana Prado, saltier and with a sharper flavor than Parmigiano-Reggiano.

Pecorino Romano is made from sheep's milk. Originating in Rome, it is a hard, white to yellowish cheese that is both dry and sharp. Aged, it is an excellent grating cheese. Its southern counterpart is Pecorino Sardo (Sardinia), sharper and saltier than Pecorino Romano. Some Pecorino cheese wheels are studded and flavored with whole black peppercorns (Pecorino Pepato).

Provolone is made from buffalo or cow's milk. It is a yellow color and can range from mild to sharp.

Ricotta is made from ewe's (adult female sheep) milk and from the whey, the residue from making other cheeses. This white cheese is very light, with a creamy, soft texture. It is a moist cheese curd similar to cottage cheese.

THE CARDINAL RULES
FOR
ITALIAN CHEESE

Fresh is best. A cut from a wheel or ball of cheese is guaranteed to more flavorful than buying what has already been cut, packaged and labeled. Wrap cut cheeses tightly with plastic wrap and refrigerate them immediately after use.

Buy only what you need and can use in about a month's time. Take out only what you need for a recipe or grate only what you will use for each meal. Some cheeses are vacuum packed, such as Gorgonzola. Once you open it, wrap it tightly with plastic wrap and refrigerate.

For cheese that has been left out of the refrigerator for some time, use a few sheets of paper toweling to absorb any condensation on the cheese before wrapping and refrigerating it. This procedure will reduce mold buildup.

Refrigerate Ricotta. Use it in two to three days, or it will become sour. If you buy ricotta in a sealed package, you can buy it well in advance of use because it will keep longer.

Provolone comes in a waxed ball and can last for months; however, once you cut into a waxed ball of Provolone, try to use it within eight to ten days.

Don't buy ready grated bottled or canned cheeses. They are guaranteed to be tasteless.

Look for the stamps on cheese wheels, such as Peccorino-Reggiano, that will guarantee both an approved and authentic product.

Use Italian soft cheeses at room temperature. For example, Gorgonzola will not only spread better, but it will taste better.

Asians are embracing Italian foods, and my experience with Asian tastes leads me to offer some special advice. If you are entertaining guests from Asia, they may find cheese difficult to digest. To some, Italian cheeses do not smell to their liking. You might wish to serve the cheese in a separate dish on the table as well as to politely inform your Asian guests about the nature of the cheese (very sharp, only a little is necessary, etc...). Because many Asians find it difficult to say no and do not wish to be impolite, you may never know whether they enjoyed the cheese or not. When in doubt, simply say, "The cheese is very strong. I think you'll like the *bruschetta* without it." Or perhaps you might suggest, "Try just a little. Some people prefer little or none at all." These suggestions will reduce embarrassment and set the stage for a more enjoyable meal.

BREAD

When I was a boy of seven or eight, I can remember especially the winter drives in our 1937 Buick to buy fresh Italian bread at the local bakery. The experience of going into the large baking room—where the bread was both baked and sold—and breathing in the aroma of freshly baked breads and pizza still lingers in my mind. Most of all, however, I remember the ride home in the cold Buick, and I used to hug the packages of warm bread to ward off the chill. Once home, it wasn't long before my two brothers and my mom and dad devoured at least one loaf. It is no wonder that today I still prefer Italian bread for my *bruschetta*.

Thus, to be authentic, I recommend that you make your *bruschetta* with Italian bread. I prefer Italian breads so much, that I even bring many loaves back to Maui from my home town in New York—Niagara Falls—from the famous DiCamillo Bakery. Canada also produces some excellent old world Italian breads.

The next best approach is to bake your own Italian bread. There are excellent books available on baking Italian breads. Head out to your favorite bookstore, pull some titles from the shelves, order a cappuccino, and leaf through them until you find one that contains recipes you want to try. Look for some of these bread recipes: Sicilian bread (round, braided, horseshoe shaped), ciabatta (slipper bread), sfilation (Italian baguette), San Francisco sourdough, pane di prato or pane Toscano (saltless Tuscan bread), pane casalingo (Italian household bread), pane Etrusca (Etruscan round loaf), and Pugliese bread (one of the better breads to use for *bruschetta*). With book in hand, head to the supermarket and home to your kitchen.

You do not necessarily have to be a purist about Italian bread. When it is unavailable, and you cannot make your own, substitute another crusty bread that is baked in your region. The search can be an adventure, and finding a good substitute will be worth the time spent.

French bread can be a good substitute, especially the baguette, pain de campagne (French sourdough), and boule; however, the center of French breads is soft, so slicing the loaves several hours ahead of toasting will allow the slices to take the pressure of rubbing the garlic better. As a rule, some French breads available in supermarkets are very soft—both the crust and the inside— and they are not readily usable for *bruschetta*; however, remove the loaves from their bags and let them sit on the kitchen counter for a few days, and then they will be ready to use. You can also re-bake them in a slow oven.

In San Francisco, I like to experiment with sourdough breads. Seattle, Chicago, New York and other large cities have many kinds of crusty breads available at bakeries, supermarkets and co-ops.

Some of these wholesome loaves are multi-grained, whole wheat, and even topped with a wide variety of seeds and grains. Others contain dried olives, coarse grains, nuts, onions, garlic, peppers, etc...

Round, hard rolls can also be used. I take a paper thin slice off the tops and bottoms, and then slice them in halves or thirds, depending on the thickness of the rolls. These nice, round slices for *bruschetta* will make an interesting display for your guests. You can also use the Italian long, hard rolls and slice them lengthwise.

Here are some other breads you can try: breads with olives, onion, garlic, or sun-dried tomatoes; dark whole wheat or black breads; breads that contain cheeses and spicy peppers; breads made with pistachios, poppy seeds, or pumpernickel; light or dark rye breads; and herb breads made with rosemary, dill, oregano, or basil.

Be a traditionalist or use your imagination.

OLIVE OIL

The first thing, among many, to say about olive oil is that it is one of the "good" oils. Olive oil is considered a "healthy" oil because it contains less saturated fat than other oils and has low ratios of omega-6 and omega-3. Olives also contain monounsaturated fats, better for your heart, and do not promote cancer. Olive oil is cholesterol free, too. We know that high fat diets promote heart disease and cancer, so using olive oil is a good choice instead of oils such as those made from coconut, safflower, and corn.

But besides considering olive oil as a healthy food, it is also a tasty one. Many Italian foods require differing grades of olive oil—made from the first to the final pressing of olives. But it is the first pressing that produces extra virgin olive oil—rich in flavor, varying from a rich amber to deep green in color, and having a delicate nutty to flowery taste.

There are five grades of olive oil: 1) Extra Virgin is the best. It results from the first cold pressing of green, ripe olives, using stone grinders. This process does not alter the oil's chemical makeup. It also contains the lowest level of acidity of all of the olive oils produced. The only downside is that it is expensive. It is best used for dressings for salads, antipasti, fish, etc., but never for cooking and frying. For *bruschetta*, you always want to use extra virgin olive oil. 2) Virgin is the next best. It has a higher acidity than extra virgin olive oil. It is good for cooking. 3) Pure comes from the third pressing, which is under heat. It is excellent for frying or cooking. 4) Light or Fine is as it suggests, light in flavor and texture. It is also good for frying and cooking. 5) Pomace comes from the final pressing, which is under extreme heat. It is frequently bitter and the cheapest. Avoid using it altogether or only as a very last resort.

Because olive oil is expensive and flavorful, you will want to treat it well. Keep your olive oil in a cool, dark place, such as in the cupboard or in an oil can (there are several available with long neck spouts for easy, dripless pouring). It will keep for up to six months. During hot summers, refrigerate it. Although it will become cloudy, when you remove the amount you will need, it will clarify at room temperature. It is best not to buy more than you will use in a short period of time. If you use it sparingly, buy a small bottle or can. If you use it regularly, purchase a larger size.

The recipes in this book list olive oil for frying. Use light or fine. Because olive oil can be heated to very high temperatures without smoking or burning, it is ideal for preparing fried foods. The recipes also call for drizzling extra virgin olive oil onto grilled or toasted Italian bread. Every penny spent on extra virgin olive oil will be well worth it when the *bruschetta* touches your palate. You are about to taste the "liquor" of the gods!

GARLIC

I grew up with garlic, both as a food and as a cure-all. Mom used it in all kinds of recipes, too many to list. When I had a serious cold, Mom strung a peeled clove of garlic on a piece of string and tied it around my neck. I'd wear it for days or even weeks, until I returned to good health. If I had some kind of internal illness, I would be given whole cloves of garlic to eat. Now, as I look back, I know why my teachers never gave me their full and "close" attention when I returned to school. During my boyhood days, the smell of garlic never bothered me. When I became a teenager, Mom advised that I chew fresh parsley before a date, and then brush my teeth well. Today, garlic is well-respected, but some people are still socially conscious about its odor.

Use only fresh garlic for *bruschetta*. You can keep garlic for several months if you store it in a cool, dry, and well-ventilated place. Avoid refrigerating it. Freezing it will destroy it. If you are lucky enough to have a cool cellar, store it there. On Maui where I live, I store my garlic in a large, uncovered ceramic bowl on the kitchen counter, away from any heat sources. It keeps well for up to two months. Then I replenish my supply.

Select garlic that is firm and without blemishes, darkened or soft spots. Look for bulbs with large cloves, especially since they are easier to hold when rubbing toast for *bruschetta*. Color can range from silver, with a papery skin to those striped with red or blue. In the United States, the most common garlic is grown in California, a softneck variety that has a white skin. Last of all, avoid using "elephant" garlic. Although you may see it in the supermarket labeled as garlic, it is not a garlic at all.

To remove the skins, you can use one of the rubber rollers available in kitchen stores. You can also drop the cloves into boiling water for ten seconds to loosen the skins. I prefer the old-fashioned way, and simply use a sharp paring knife to trim each end and peel off the skins. If you are using the second method for making *bruschetta*, that is making a garlic paste with olive oil, then you can crush the cloves of garlic. Place the flat side of a knife blade over each clove and then either press hard or give the blade a crack with the bottom part of your closed fist. The skin will come loose and can be removed easily with your fingers or with a small knife.

When applying the garlic to the toast, experiment by rubbing gently, hard or somewhere in-between. Go over the bread once. Try it twice if you prefer. But experiment enough to find out the right amount of garlic for your taste. At first, your enthusiasm my result in using a lot of garlic. My preference is not to overdo it, and I go over the bread lightly and only once.

VARIATIONS, SUBSTITUTIONS & REPETITION

I have included food variations and substitutions in some cases when certain items may not be available locally. For example, walnuts have been suggested as a substitute for pine nuts, and a variety of greens is suggested in place of dandelions. Regardless, feel free to use your own imagination when one or another food item is not available in your region. In fact, you may end up creating a very unique and tasty *bruschetta* by using a substitute. In Hawai'i and on Maui where I live, one might experiment with unsalted macadamia nuts in place of pine nuts, and choi sum in place of dandelions. Variations and substitutions are endless.

I always find substituting both a challenge and a creative process at the same time. I try to use different food items or search local and Mainland stores to add to my well-stocked pantry. There is always something new or different that catches my eye and excites my palate. Whether I am in Seattle, San Francisco, Chicago or New York, I take great pleasure in searching out items that will create unique and tasty *bruschetta*. Good hunting!

Besides being comfortable with food substitutions, I am also flexible about the preparation of foods. As a general rule, I do not follow the instructions of every recipe exactly. A case in point is my insistence on mincing with a knife on a wood cutting board, or when making bread or pizza dough, I prefer doing it by hand rather than using a food processor or a bread machine.

Every cook has his or her own way of doing things. My preference is not to use electric cutters, food processors, etc.... I enjoy the tactile approach, and I like to see my food being prepared and judged "just right" by feel and eye. In addition, I enjoy the length of time it takes to prepare food. I get a good feeling when I know that my time has played an important role in making the result a joy for my guests' palates. There are, however, a few recipes for toppings where I have included using an appliance, so I am not altogether a purist.

Regardless of my preferences, feel free to substitute foods or to use any variation that pleases you. And don't feel guilty about it. There are two exceptions—substitutions for the genuine flavors of fresh garlic and extra virgin olive oil. Although garlic is now available in juice form, in powders, flakes and granules, salted, minced, pickled, and even in sprays, I do not recommend them in place of the real thing. As I said before, I am not a purist. One of my recipes calls for garlic powder! Second, don't skimp on olive oil. There is no substitute for high quality, extra virgin olive oil. It costs more, but your *bruschetta* deserves it and your guests will know you care about them!

Finally, because I dislike recipes in cookbooks that continually refer the reader to different pages for instructions or ingredients, the recipes in *SIMPLY BRUSCHETTA—Garlic Toast the Italian Way* have been written to stand alone. Although the reader will sense some repetition, the fully complete one-page recipes are more user-friendly. Once you open the book to prepare any recipe, everything you need to know is right there. *Buon appetito!*

BRUSCHETTA

Traditional Bruschetta Con Aglio	Shallots and Tomato
Pesto	Olive
Pepper Rainbow	Chicken Liver Pâté
Broccoli Rabe	Spinach and Egg
Oregano, Tomato and Onion	Fried Polenta Sans Toast
Anchovy	Three Peppercorns
Gorgonzola and Red Onion	Egg and Cheese
Anise	Marinated Eggplant
Marinara Sauce	Green Tomato
Sun-Dried Tomato	Asparagus
Roma Plum Tomato and Basil	Fava
Red Chili Pepper	Fried Onions and Green Peppers
Italian Sausage, Peppers and Onions	Bone Marrow
Portabella Mushroom	Sardines and Lemon
Roasted Garlic	Drowned Bruschetta
Prosciutto and Melon	Fried Cardoon
Mixed Greens	Tomato, Anchovy and Scallions
Salmon and Capers	Broccolini
Pine Nuts, Currants and Tomato	Finocchio and Pimiento
Roasted Peppers	Beans and Greens
Tomato and Oregano	Fried Mozzarella
Zucchini	Roma Plum Tomato Rub
Orange and Anchovy	Chestnut
Grilled Tomato	Caponata
Sweet Caribe Banana Pepper	Arugula and Plum Tomato
Ricotta and Olive	Butternut Squash, Pine Nuts and Bacon
Artichoke, Roasted Pepper and Plum Tomato	Grilled Vegetables
Baked Eggplant	Artichoke, Olive and Tomato
Rosemary, Red Onion and Chili Pepper	Shredded Chicken
Dandelion Greens and Bacon	Fried Garlic
Grilled Eggplant and Mozzarella	Eggplant Spread
Cucumber and Balsamic Vinegar	Salmon, Tomato and Onion
Artichoke	Finale

TRADITIONAL BRUSCHETTA CON AGLIO

Once you have been given your wings,
remember that there are many different kinds of winds. . .

INGREDIENTS

8 one inch thick slices of Italian bread, 2 - 3 days old
1 or 2 cloves of garlic
1/3 - 1/2 cup of extra virgin olive oil
sea salt

PREPARATION

1 Peel one or two cloves of garlic (uncrushed).
2 Cut eight one-inch thick slices of Italian bread.
3 Charcoal grill both sides. (See VARIATIONS below).
4 Remove the grilled bread to a platter.
5 While the slices are still hot, rub the garlic back and forth over the entire surface, including the crust.
6 Drizzle extra virgin olive oil onto each slice, or using a pastry brush, spread the olive oil onto each slice.
7 Use a grinder to sprinkle coarse sea salt to taste onto each slice.

VARIATIONS

If you do not have a charcoal grill, use an oven to broil both sides or use a toaster oven or a wide-slice toaster to toast the bread.
Substitute another crusty bread.
Lightly sprinkle grated Pecorino Romano cheese on top of each slice. Reduce the amount of sea salt.
Lightly sprinkle fresh or dried oregano on top of each slice.
Sprinkle freshly ground black peppercorns, to taste.
Use regular salt.
Use balsamic vinegar as a dip for the *bruschetta con aglio*.

IMPORTANT NOTE

Traditional *Bruschetta Con Aglio* is the core recipe for most of the following recipes in *SIMPLY BRUSCHETTA—Garlic Toast the Italian Way*. Any variations are explained in each recipe.

PESTO

Without tradition, we find the threads of this, that, and the next world
dissolve. . .
our connections are threatened and our identity becomes meaningless.
Thank God for bruschetta!

INGREDIENTS

8 half inch thick slices of Italian bread, 2 - 3 days old
2 large cloves of garlic
1/3 - 1/2 cup of extra virgin olive oil
1 cup of fresh basil leaves (packed)
1/4 cup of pine nuts
1/4 cup of grated Parmigiano-Reggiano cheese
sea salt and black peppercorns

PREPARATION

1 Crush and then peel two large cloves of garlic.
2 Using a mortar and pestle, blend and mash the garlic until it is pasty.
3 Chop the pine nuts very fine and blend with the garlic paste.
4 Chop the basil very fine and blend with the garlic and pine nuts.
5 Add olive oil a little at a time. Continue to blend the ingredients.
6 Blend in the grated Parmigiano-Reggiano cheese.
7 Add sea salt and freshly ground black peppercorns to taste.
8 Place the mixture in a small pot and heat it until it is lightly warmed. Stir frequently.
9 Charcoal grill, broil or toast both sides of eight slices of Italian bread.
10 While the bread is still hot, spread the warmed mixture over the entire surface, including the crust.

VARIATIONS

Toast the pine nuts.
Use walnuts or chestnuts.
Use Pecorino Romano cheese. Omit or reduce the salt.
Substitute dried basil.
Use the spread at room temperature.
Substitute fresh parsley, rosemary, dill, mint, or another favorite fresh herb.

PEPPER RAINBOW

*It is the shape of one thing that creates
the shape of another. . .*

INGREDIENTS

8 half inch thick slices of Italian bread, 2 - 3 days old
1 or 2 cloves of garlic
1/3 - 1/2 cup of extra virgin olive oil
1 each (medium size) green, red, yellow, purple bell peppers
1/2 cup of light olive oil for frying
sea salt

PREPARATION

1   Halve the peppers and remove the stems and seeds. Then slice them into thin strips, about one
    inch wide. Wash, drain and pat dry with paper toweling. Fry on medium-high heat in one half
    cup of light olive oil until soft and lightly browned.
2   Peel one or two cloves of garlic (uncrushed).
3   Charcoal grill, broil or toast both sides of eight slices of Italian bread.
4   While the slices are still hot, rub the garlic back and forth over the entire surface, including the crust.
5   Combine the olive oil left over from frying the peppers with the extra virgin olive oil and drizzle
    onto each slice, or using a pastry brush, spread the oil mixture onto each slice.
6   Place the strips of fried peppers, grouping them by color, onto each slice to create a rainbow
    effect. Refrigerate any of the remaining peppers for future use.
7   Add sea salt to taste.

VARIATIONS

Use at least green and red peppers or at least two peppers of any other color combination.
Use any peppers in season (mild or hot).
Place peppers diagonally on the toast.

BROCCOLI RABE

Sometimes the best part of a recipe
is what you leave out. . .

INGREDIENTS

8 half inch thick slices of Italian bread, 2 - 3 days old
1 or 2 cloves of garlic
1/3 - 1/2 cup of extra virgin olive oil
1 bunch of broccoli rabe (rapini)
2 tablespoons of extra virgin olive oil
sea salt and black peppercorns

PREPARATION

1 Cut the broccoli rabe in three inch lengths. Wash and drain. Put in a Pyrex dish with one third cup of water and cover with plastic wrap. Microwave for about four minutes. Time may vary depending on the power and setting of the microwave.
2 Remove broccoli rabe. Drain well in a colander.
3 Peel one or two cloves of garlic (uncrushed).
4 Charcoal grill, broil or toast both sides of eight slices of Italian bread.
5 While the slices are still hot, rub the garlic back and forth over the entire surface, including the crust.
6 Drizzle extra virgin olive oil onto each slice, or using a pastry brush, spread the olive oil onto each slice.
7 Spoon on the broccoli rabe. Lightly drizzle two tablespoons of olive oil over the broccoli rabe.
8 Add sea salt and freshly ground black peppercorns to taste.

VARIATIONS

Substitute broccoli.
Substitute broccolini.
Sprinkle grated Pecorino Romano cheese on top.

OREGANO, TOMATO AND ONION

*Although your mother may no longer be with you,
she still resides in the foods you prepare.
and for many generations henceforth. . .*

INGREDIENTS

8 half inch thick slices of Italian bread, 2 - 3 days old
1 or 2 cloves of garlic
1/3 - 1/2 cup of extra virgin olive oil
1 one pound 12 ounce can of peeled whole tomatoes
1 medium Spanish onion
2 tablespoons of fresh oregano
sea salt and black peppercorns

PREPARATION

1 Drain the juice from the can of tomatoes, slice them in half, and squeeze out the seeds.
2 In a bowl, lightly mash the tomatoes with your hands. Add them to a pot and warm on low heat. Drain again to remove excess liquid.
3 Peel one or two cloves of garlic.
4 Charcoal grill, broil or toast both sides of eight slices of Italian bread.
5 While the slices are still hot, rub the garlic back and forth over the entire surface, including the crust.
6 Drizzle extra virgin olive oil onto each slice, or using a pastry brush, spread the olive oil onto each slice.
7 Spoon the warmed tomato mixture onto each slice.
8 Top with finely chopped onion and sprinkle with fresh oregano.
9 Add sea salt and freshly ground black peppercorns to taste.

VARIATIONS

Lightly sprinkle grated Pecorino Romano cheese on top of each slice.
Use dried oregano.
Use red onion, Maui onion, Kula onion, Vedalia onion, or scallions.
Spoon tomato mixture onto slices at room temperature.

ANCHOVY

When you come to my home, I insist, "Eat. . . drink. . ."
I want you to leave with more than just simple hospitality.
I want you to taste it.

INGREDIENTS

8 half inch thick slices of Italian bread, 2 - 3 days old
1 or 2 cloves of garlic
1/3 - 1/2 cup of extra virgin olive oil
1 two ounce can of anchovy fillets
1 medium sweet onion
black peppercorns

PREPARATION

1 Peel one or two cloves of garlic.
2 Charcoal grill, broil or toast both sides of eight slices of Italian bread.
3 While the slices are still hot, rub the garlic back and forth over the entire surface, including the crust.
4 Drizzle extra virgin olive oil onto each slice, or using a pastry brush, spread the olive oil onto each slice.
5 Drain the oil from the anchovies.
6 Place two or three anchovies diagonally across each slice and top with finely chopped onions.
7 Add freshly ground black peppercorns to taste.

VARIATIONS

Instead of using whole anchovies, mash them with the oil from the can and spread this mixture onto each slice.
Combine the oil from the can of anchovies with the olive oil and drizzle onto each slice.
Add chopped vine ripened Roma plum tomatoes.
Sprinkle with fresh or dried oregano.

GORGONZOLA AND RED ONION

I made it perfect, but without a flaw it saddened me. . .

INGREDIENTS

8 half inch thick slices of Italian bread, 2 - 3 days old
1 or 2 cloves of garlic
1/3 - 1/2 cup of extra virgin olive oil
1 small red onion (purple skinned)
6 ounces of Gorgonzola cheese
black peppercorns

PREPARATION

1 Peel one or two cloves of garlic (uncrushed).
2 Mash the Gorgonzola cheese (room temperature) with a fork.
3 Charcoal grill, broil or toast both sides of eight slices of Italian bread.
4 While the slices are still hot, rub the garlic back and forth over the entire surface, including the crust.
5 Drizzle extra virgin olive oil onto each slice, or using a pastry brush, spread the olive oil onto each slice.
6 With a knife or a spatula, spread a thin layer of Gorgonzola cheese (room temperature) onto each slice.
7 Add finely chopped red onion.
8 Add freshly ground black peppercorn.

VARIATIONS

Use blue cheese.
Use Spanish onion, Maui onion, Kula onion, or Vedalia onion.
Sprinkle with bits of crispy fried bacon.

ANISE

Sometimes the greatest search for the best combination of tastes happens by accident. . .
Then we ask, "What did we do right. . . or wrong?"

INGREDIENTS

8 half inch thick slices of Italian bread, 2 - 3 days old
2 cloves of garlic
1/3 - 1/2 cup of extra virgin olive oil
1 tablespoon of dried anise seed
1 cup of grated Mozzarella cheese
1/2 teaspoon of sea salt
black peppercorns

PREPARATION

1   Using a mortar and pestle, crush and grind the anise to a fine consistency. Using a tea strainer, separate the anise from the anise shells. Discard the shells.
2   Crush and then peel two cloves of garlic. Mash and blend them with the anise until pasty.
3   Add one half teaspoon of sea salt.
4   Add olive oil a little at a time. Continue to mash and blend the ingredients until smooth.
5   Charcoal grill, broil or toast both sides of eight slices of Italian bread.
6   While the slices are still hot, spread the mixture over the entire surface, including the crust.
7   Sprinkle each slice with grated Mozzarella cheese.
8   Add freshly ground black peppercorns to taste.

VARIATIONS

Use Parmigiano-Reggiano cheese.
Substitute anise oil.
Broil until cheese melts.

MARINARA SAUCE

If you cannot reach her with words,
try to touch her with your sauce. . .

INGREDIENTS

8 half inch thick slices of Italian bread, 2 - 3 days old
1 or 2 cloves of garlic
1/3 - 1/2 cup of extra virgin olive oil
1 tablespoon of fresh oregano
1/4 cup of Pecorino Romano cheese
2 cups of marinara sauce

PREPARATION

1 Put the marinara sauce (either home made or prepared) in a small pot and warm it on low heat.
2 Peel one or two cloves of garlic (uncrushed).
3 Charcoal grill, broil or toast both sides of eight slices of Italian bread.
4 While the slices are still hot, rub the garlic back and forth over the entire surface, including the crust.
5 Drizzle extra virgin olive oil onto each slice, or using a pastry brush, spread the olive oil onto each slice.
6 Spoon an even layer of the warmed marinara sauce onto each slice.
7 Add fresh oregano and grated Pecorino Romano cheese.

VARIATIONS

Add thinly sliced meatballs on top.
Use dried oregano.
Substitute other sauces made with peppers, mushrooms, eggplant, etc...

SUN~DRIED TOMATO

*Observe the movement of chefs' hands,
and you will see them thinking. . . creating. . .*

INGREDIENTS

8 half inch thick slices of Italian bread, 2 - 3 days old
2 cloves of garlic
1/3 - 1/2 cup of extra virgin olive oil
3 dozen slices (small) of sun-dried red tomatoes
1/2 cup of fresh basil
1/2 teaspoon of sea salt
1/4 cup of grated Pecorino Romano cheese
black peppercorns

PREPARATION

1 Soak the slices of sun-dried tomatoes in one cup of hot water for ten minutes. Drain and pat dry with paper towels. Chop (coarse).
2 Crush and then peel two cloves of garlic. Using a mortar and pestle, blend and mash the garlic until it is pasty.
3 Add the tomatoes and blend with the garlic paste.
4 Chop the basil leaves very fine and blend with the garlic and tomatoes.
5 Add olive oil a little at a time. Add the sea salt. Continue to mix the ingredients until blended well.
6 Charcoal grill, broil or toast both sides of eight slices of Italian bread.
7 While the bread is still hot, use a pastry brush to spread the mixture over the entire surface, including the crust.
8 Spoon the sun-dried tomato mixture onto each slice.
9 Sprinkle with grated Pecorino Romano cheese.
10 Add freshly ground black peppercorns to taste.

VARIATIONS

Use yellow sun-dried tomatoes.
Use dried basil.
Use Parmigiano-Reggiano cheese.
Use oregano instead of basil.

ROMA PLUM TOMATO AND BASIL

God gave us the tomato, and modern day scientists have perfected its looks, increased its shelf life, and destroyed its flavor. Grow your own!

INGREDIENTS

8 half inch thick slices of Italian bread, 2 - 3 days old
1 or 2 cloves of garlic
1/3 - 1/2 cup of extra virgin olive oil
8 vine ripened Roma plum tomatoes
1 dozen leaves of fresh basil
1/4 cup of balsamic vinegar
2/3 cup of Mozzarella cheese
1/2 teaspoon of sea salt
black peppercorns

PREPARATION

1 Bring two quarts of water to a boil. Add Roma plum tomatoes and scald for one minute. Put them into a pan of water and ice to stop them from cooking. Remove the skins.
2 Cut the tomatoes in half, (removing seeds is optional), and place them into a deep bowl. Squeeze the tomatoes with your hands to create a pulp-like consistency. Drain off any liquid. Add basil, chopped fine, balsamic vinegar, sea salt, and freshly ground black peppercorns, to taste. Mix well and let stand for fifteen minutes.
3 Peel one or two cloves of garlic (uncrushed).
4 Charcoal grill, broil or toast both sides of eight slices of Italian bread.
5 While the slices are still hot, rub the garlic back and forth over the entire surface, including the crust.
6 Drizzle extra virgin olive oil onto each slice, or using a pastry brush, spread the olive oil onto each slice.
7 Spoon and spread the tomato mixture onto each slice.
8 Sprinkle with grated Mozzarella cheese. Place slices on an ungreased baking sheet and broil in an oven, about four inches from the heating element until the cheese melts and becomes lightly browned.

VARIATIONS

Use jack or white cheddar cheese.
Use another tomato of choice or substitute canned tomatoes.
Sprinkle finely chopped onions on top before adding cheese.

RED CHILI PEPPER

*If I sit down to join you for dinner
and do not speak, do not assume
that I am not enjoying your good food and company. . .*

INGREDIENTS

8 half inch thick slices of Italian bread, 2 - 3 days old
1 or 2 cloves of garlic
1/3 - 1/2 cup of extra virgin olive oil
2 teaspoons of dried hot, red chili pepper flakes
sea salt

PREPARATION

1   Peel one or two cloves of garlic (uncrushed).
2   Charcoal grill, broil or toast both sides of eight slices of Italian bread.
3   While the slices are still hot, rub the garlic back and forth over the entire surface, including the crust.
4   Drizzle extra virgin olive oil onto each slice, or using a pastry brush, spread the olive oil onto each slice.
5   Sprinkle each slice with dried hot, red chili pepper flakes.
6   Add sea salt to taste.

VARIATIONS

Use any dried chili pepper, mild, medium or hot.
Make or use a prepared chili pepper paste.
Lightly sprinkle Pecorino Romano cheese on top of each slice. Omit or reduce salt.

ITALIAN SAUSAGE, PEPPERS AND ONION

Bruschetta without wine is like the sky without the sun. . .

INGREDIENTS

8 half inch slices of Italian bread, 2 - 3 days old
1 or 2 cloves of garlic
1/3 - 1/2 cup of extra virgin olive oil
4 Italian sausages (select mild, medium or hot)
1/2 green bell pepper
1/2 red bell pepper
2 tablespoons olive oil for frying
1 medium onion
1/2 teaspoon of salt
sea salt and black peppercorns

PREPARATION

1 Heat two tablespoons of olive oil on medium. Add the sausage and cook thoroughly and until it is browned. Half way through cooking, prick each sausage several times with a fork or sharp tipped knife to release the juices. Cooking time will vary depending on size and thickness.
2 Once the sausages are cooked, remove them to a cutting board to cool.
3 Slice the bell peppers into strips. Cut the onion in half and then slice into very thin pieces. Add the bell peppers, onion and salt to the remaining oil used to fry the sausages. Cook on medium to high heat until soft and lightly browned.
4 Cut the sausages into quarters lengthwise and then slice them into small cubes. Add them to the peppers and onions and fry another five minutes. Toss frequently. Remove to a bowl.
5 Peel one or two large cloves of garlic.
6 Charcoal grill, broil or toast eight slices of Italian bread.
7 While the slices are still hot, rub the garlic back and forth over the entire surface, including the crust.
8 Drizzle extra virgin olive oil onto each slice, or using a pastry brush, spread the olive oil onto each slice.
9 Spoon on generous amounts of the sausage and vegetable mixture.
10 Sprinkle on sea salt and fresh ground peppercorns to taste (optional).

VARIATIONS

Substitute other peppers in season, mild or hot, according to taste.

PORTABELLA MUSHROOM

There is little room for me to roam,
but I have traveled far and wide with recipes from my cookbooks. . .

INGREDIENTS

8 half inch thick slices of Italian bread, 2 - 3 days old
1 or 2 cloves of garlic
1/3 - 1/2 cup of extra virgin olive oil
1 large portabella mushroom
1 medium onion
1/2 teaspoon of salt
2 tablespoons of olive oil for frying
6 ounces of Mozzarella cheese
sea salt and black peppercorns

PREPARATION

1 Wash, cut, and chop the portabella mushroom (coarse).
2 Peel and cut the onion into very thin slices.
3 Add one tablespoon of olive oil to a skillet and fry the mushrooms and onions with one half teaspoon of salt on medium to high heat. After about five minutes, use a spoon to remove any juices that have been released. Then add one more tablespoon of olive oil and continue to fry another five minutes or until the mixture becomes soft and lightly browned.
4 Peel one or two cloves of garlic (uncrushed).
5 Charcoal grill, broil or toast both sides of eight slices of Italian bread.
6 While the slices are still hot, rub the garlic back and forth over the entire surface, including the crust.
7 Drizzle extra virgin olive oil onto each slice, or using a pastry brush, spread the olive oil onto each slice.
8 Place the toasted slices on an ungreased baking sheet. Spoon and then spread equal amounts of the mushroom and onion mixture onto each slice of toast.
9 Place three rectangular slices of Mozzarella cheese diagonally onto each slice and sprinkle with freshly ground black peppercorns to taste. Broil in an oven, about four inches from the heating element until the cheese melts and becomes lightly browned.

VARIATIONS

Lightly sprinkle Pecorino Romano cheese on top of each slice in place of Mozzarella.
Substitute one third of a pound of shiitake, morel, chanterelle, porcini, or trompettes des morts.

ROASTED GARLIC

*A meal is frequently accompanied by a toast
for good health and long life. . .
At the same time, do we realize
that how long we live is less important than how we live?*

INGREDIENTS

8 half inch thick slices of Italian bread, 2 - 3 days old
2 large bulbs of garlic
1/3 - 1/2 cup of extra virgin olive oil
1/3 cup of Fontinella cheese
1/2 teaspoon of salt
black peppercorns

PREPARATION

1 Cut the top off of each bulb of garlic to expose the tops of the cloves.
2 Rub olive oil on the unpeeled surface and drizzle oil on the top.
3 Wrap in aluminum foil. Punch holes in the foil with a fork, and place in a small Pyrex dish. Bake for forty-five minutes to one hour at 375 degrees. Time may vary depending on the kind of oven that is used and the size of the garlic bulbs. The garlic is fully cooked when it becomes soft and mushy.
4 Remove from the oven and allow to cool. Then squeeze the roasted garlic from each clove into a bowl. Add the olive oil and salt. Blend with a fork.
5 Charcoal grill, broil or toast both sides of eight slices of Italian bread.
6 Spread the baked garlic, olive oil and salt mixture onto each slice.
7 Place a thin layer of thinly sliced or grated Fontinella cheese on each slice.
8 Add freshly ground black peppercorns to taste.

VARIATIONS

Use Provolone, Fontina or Mozzarella cheese.
Omit cheese.

PROSCIUTTO AND MELON

*To nourish our physical selves and to raise our spirits,
we depend on a kind of death that brings new life.
Do we not uproot vegetables and eat the flesh of animals?*

INGREDIENTS

8 half inch thick slices of Italian bread, 2 - 3 days old
1 or 2 cloves of garlic
1/3 - 1/2 cup of extra virgin olive oil
8 paper thin slices of prosciutto
1/3 section of cantaloupe

PREPARATION

1   Peel one or two cloves of garlic (uncrushed).
2   Charcoal grill, broil or toast both sides of eight slices of Italian bread.
3   While the slices are still hot, rub the garlic back and forth over the entire surface, including the crust.
4   Drizzle extra virgin olive oil onto each slice, or using a pastry brush, spread the olive oil onto each slice.
5   Arrange thin slices of prosciutto on each piece of toast and top with very thin slices of cantaloupe.
6   Peel and seed the cantaloupe. Cut into very thin slices and place on top of the prosciutto.

VARIATIONS

Alternate slices of melon and prosciutto.
Use another kind of fresh melon in season.
Add thin slices of Provolone.
Add freshly ground black peppercorns.
Substitute thinly sliced boiled ham for prosciutto.

MIXED GREENS

When I was a child,
I refused to eat some of our traditional Italian foods.
Today, I can't get enough!

INGREDIENTS

8 half inch slices of Italian bread, 2 - 3 days old
1 or 2 cloves of garlic
1/3 - 1/2 cup of extra virgin olive oil
2 or 3 leaves each of fresh endive, arugula, dandelions, and romaine
1 tablespoon of extra virgin olive oil
1 1/2 tablespoons of balsamic vinegar
salt

PREPARATION

1 Wash the endive, arugula, dandelions, and romaine leaves. Spin dry in a salad spinner or pat dry with paper toweling.
2 Tear leaves into very small pieces and discard spines. Put in a large salad bowl.
3 Add one tablespoon of extra virgin olive oil, balsamic vinegar, and salt to taste. Toss lightly to coat greens.
4 Peel one or two cloves of garlic.
5 Charcoal grill, broil or toast eight slices of Italian bread.
6 While the slices are still hot, rub the garlic back and forth over the entire surface, including the crust.
7 Drizzle extra virgin olive oil onto each slice, or using a pastry brush, spread the olive oil onto each slice.
8 Cover each slice with the mixed greens and serve.

VARIATIONS

Add fresh basil.
Substitute other fresh greens in season.
Add other vegetables, such as diced Roma plum tomato and chopped onions.

SALMON AND CAPERS

When you think you have found the best recipe, you haven't. . .
Each new time you prepare a dish,
it can change in a myriad of ways.

INGREDIENTS

8 half inch thick slices of Italian bread, 2 - 3 days old
1 or 2 cloves of garlic
1/3 - 1/2 cup of extra virgin olive oil
1/3 pound of very thin sliced smoked salmon
1 small jar of capers
4 scallions
black peppercorns

PREPARATION

1 Peel one or two cloves of garlic (uncrushed).
2 Charcoal grill, broil or toast both sides of eight slices of Italian bread.
3 While the slices are still hot, rub the garlic back and forth over the entire surface, including the crust.
4 Drizzle extra virgin olive oil onto each slice, or using a pastry brush, spread the olive oil onto each slice.
5 Arrange thin slices of smoked salmon on each piece of toast and top with several capers (drained well).
6 Sprinkle with chopped scallions and freshly ground black peppercorns to taste.

VARIATIONS

Use canned salmon. Drain well.
Use chopped onions, leeks or chives.
Use loks.

PINE NUTS, CURRANTS AND TOMATO

An antipasto is geometry and art. . . motionless on a platter,
but dancing in front of our eyes and exciting our palates. . .

INGREDIENTS

8 half inch thick slices of Italian bread, 2 - 3 days old
1 or 2 cloves of garlic
1/3 - 1/2 cup of extra virgin olive oil
1/2 cup pine nuts
4 vine ripened Roma plum tomatoes
1/4 cup fresh basil leaves
1/2 cup dried currants
sea salt and black peppercorns

PREPARATION

1 Toast the pine nuts in a pan under a broiler until lightly browned. Toss the nuts periodically to toast them evenly. Time will vary.
2 Slice the Roma plum tomatoes in half, squeeze out the juice, and remove the seeds. Chop them into large pieces.
3 Cut the basil leaves into strips.
4 Peel one or two cloves of garlic.
5 Charcoal grill, broil or toast both sides of eight slices of Italian bread.
6 While the slices are still hot, rub the garlic back and forth over the entire surface, including the crust.
7 Drizzle extra virgin olive oil onto each slice, or using a pastry brush, spread the olive oil onto each slice.
8 First spoon on the tomato, followed by a sprinkling of currants and toasted pine nuts. Top with the basil, sea salt and freshly ground peppercorns.

VARIATIONS

Use walnuts.
Use macadamia nuts.

ROASTED PEPPERS

You cannot rush good food. . .

INGREDIENTS

8 half inch thick slices of Italian bread, 2 - 3 days old
4 cloves of garlic
1/3 - 1/2 cup of extra virgin olive oil
1 twelve ounce bottle of sweet roasted red peppers (Mancini brand)
1/4 cup extra virgin olive oil
sea salt

PREPARATION

1 Peel one or two cloves of garlic (uncrushed).
2 Place the prepared peppers in a colander and drain off the excess liquid. Slice in lengths the width of the bread slices.
3 Marinate and refrigerate peppers for one day in one quarter cup of extra virgin olive oil, two cloves of garlic (crushed), and salt to taste.
4 Charcoal grill, broil or toast both sides of eight slices of Italian bread.
5 While the slices are still hot, rub the garlic back and forth over the entire surface, including the crust.
6 Drizzle extra virgin olive oil onto each slice, or using a pastry brush, spread the olive oil onto each slice.
7 Place a layer of previously marinated roasted red peppers (room temperature) on each slice of toasted bread.
8 Add sea salt to taste.

VARIATIONS

Use prepared green peppers.
Use peppers in season. Roast them under a broiler. Turn frequently. Cool and remove skins. Then marinate and refrigerate peppers for one day in one quarter cup of olive oil seasoned with two large cloves of garlic (crushed), and salt to taste.

TOMATO AND OREGANO

When you prepare foods,
remember that a series of failures can lead to success. . .

INGREDIENTS

8 half inch thick slices of Italian bread, 2 - 3 days old
1 or 2 cloves of garlic
1/3 - 1/2 cup of extra virgin olive oil
4 vine ripened Roma plum tomatoes
1 tablespoon of dried oregano
2 tablespoons of extra virgin olive oil
black peppercorns

PREPARATION

1 Bring two quarts of water to a boil. Add the Roma plum tomatoes and scald for one minute. Put them into a pan of water and ice to stop them from cooking. Remove the skins and slice them very thin.
2 Peel one or two cloves of garlic (uncrushed).
3 Charcoal grill, broil or toast both sides of eight slices of Italian bread.
4 While the slices are still hot, rub the garlic back and forth over the entire surface, including the crust.
5 Drizzle extra virgin olive oil onto each slice, or using a pastry brush, spread the olive oil onto each slice.
6 Layer the thin slices of tomato, drizzle lightly with two tablespoons of extra virgin olive oil, and sprinkle with dried oregano.
7 Add sea salt and freshly ground peppercorns to taste.

VARIATIONS

Use another kind of tomato in season. After scalding and peeling, remove some of the seeds and squeeze to remove excess juice.
Top with chopped onions.
Use fresh oregano.
Sprinkle with Parmigiano-Reggiano cheese.

ZUCCHINI

*If you want to know my heart,
partake in my food.*

INGREDIENTS

8 half inch thick slices of Italian bread, 2 - 3 days old
1 or 2 cloves of garlic
1/3 - 1/2 cup of extra virgin olive oil
3 medium zucchini
1/2 cup of flour
1 teaspoon of salt
2 cups of light olive oil for frying
sea salt and black peppercorns

PREPARATION

1   Cut zucchini into very thin (round) slices, about one eighth of an inch or less. Toss them in a paper bag filled with flour, one teaspoon of salt, and freshly ground black peppercorns.
2   In a deep fryer or a nonstick, six-inch skillet, quick fry the zucchini in light olive oil. Remove and drain on paper toweling.
3   Peel one or two cloves of garlic (uncrushed).
4   Charcoal grill, broil or toast both sides of eight slices of Italian bread.
5   While the slices are still hot, rub the garlic back and forth over the entire surface, including the crust.
6   Drizzle extra virgin olive oil onto each slice, or using a pastry brush, spread the olive oil onto each slice.
7   Layer the fried zucchini chips on each slice.
8   Sprinkle with sea salt.

VARIATIONS

Sprinkle with grated Pecorino Romano cheese.
Use yellow zucchini.
Drizzle additional olive oil on top of fried zucchini.
Cut zucchini lengthwise or at an angle to create larger slices.

ORANGE AND ANCHOVY

After I returned home, I knew I had changed.
But Mama's cooking hadn't,
and the anchovies were stored in the same place.

INGREDIENTS

8 half inch thick slices of Italian bread, 2 - 3 days old
1 or 2 cloves of garlic
1/3 - 1/2 cup of extra virgin olive oil
3 seedless navel oranges
2 tablespoons of extra virgin olive oil
1 two ounce can of anchovy fillets (drained)
2 tablespoons of balsamic vinegar
black peppercorns

PREPARATION

1 Peel and cut seedless oranges into thin slices, about a quarter of an inch. Marinate for two hours in their own juice, two tablespoons of extra virgin olive oil, and a generous amount of freshly ground black peppercorns.
2 Peel one or two cloves of garlic (uncrushed).
3 Charcoal grill, broil or toast both sides of eight slices of Italian bread.
4 While the slices are still hot, rub the garlic back and forth over the entire surface, including the crust.
5 Drizzle extra virgin olive oil onto each slice, or using a pastry brush, spread the olive oil onto each slice.
6 Drain the oranges, and place two or three slices onto each piece of toast.
7 Sprinkle the oranges with two tablespoons of balsamic vinegar.
8 Add two or three anchovies, placed diagonally on each slice.
9 Sprinkle with freshly ground black peppercorns.

VARIATIONS

Substitute fresh tangerines. Remove the seeds.

GRILLED TOMATO

*To an Italian, the food trinity is simply
bread, wine and cheese. . .*

INGREDIENTS

8 half inch thick slices of Italian bread, 2 - 3 days old
1 or 2 cloves of garlic
1/3 - 1/2 cup of extra virgin olive oil
3 large firm vine ripened Roma plum tomatoes
1/4 cup of bread crumbs
1/4 cup of grated Pecorino Romano cheese
1/4 cup of basil
1/4 cup of parsley
1 tablespoon of extra virgin olive oil
sea salt and black peppercorns

PREPARATION

1 Slice the Roma plum tomatoes very thick, about three quarters of an inch, and grill both sides
   on a charcoal grill.
2 In a deep bowl, mix the bread crumbs, grated Pecorino Romano cheese, the basil and parsley,
   (chopped very fine), sea salt and freshly ground black peppercorns to taste. Add one tablespoon
   of extra virgin olive oil and mix lightly with a fork so that the oil coats the ingredients.
3 Peel one or two cloves of garlic.
4 Charcoal grill, broil or toast both sides of eight slices of Italian bread.
5 While the slices are still hot, rub the garlic back and forth over the entire surface, including the crust.
6 Drizzle extra virgin olive oil onto each slice, or using a pastry brush, spread the olive oil onto
   each slice.
7 Place two slices of grilled tomatoes on each slice of toast.
8 Sprinkle the bread crumb, cheese, and spice mixture on top of the tomatoes.

VARIATIONS

Grill tomatoes in a skillet, on a stove top grill, or on a pancake griddle coated with olive oil.
Sprinkle with grated Parmigiano-Reggiano cheese.

SWEET CARIBE BANANA PEPPER

When I express that I love you,
I frequently say it with the foods I prepare for you. . .

INGREDIENTS

8 half inch thick slices of Italian bread, 2 - 3 days old
1 or 2 cloves of garlic
1/3 - 1/2 cup of extra virgin olive oil
8 large sweet caribe banana peppers
1/2 cup of light olive oil for frying
sea salt

PREPARATION

1 Slice peppers into quarters lengthwise and remove the seeds. Wash, drain, and dry well with paper toweling.
2 Fry both sides of the peppers in a skillet in one half cup of light olive oil until lightly browned and soft.
3 Peel one or two cloves of garlic (uncrushed).
4 Charcoal grill, broil or toast both sides of eight slices of Italian bread.
5 While the slices are still hot, rub the garlic back and forth over the entire surface, including the crust.
6 Drizzle extra virgin olive oil onto each slice, or using a pastry brush, spread the olive oil onto each slice.
7 Place four fried pepper quarters onto each slice.
8 Add sea salt to taste.

VARIATIONS

Use any other sweet pepper in season.
Substitute a hot pepper of choice.
Combine the olive oil left over from frying peppers with the extra virgin olive oil and drizzle onto each slice.

RICOTTA AND OLIVE

When we focus too hard on perfection,
something gets lost from the recipe. . .

INGREDIENTS

8 half inch thick slices of Italian bread, 2 - 3 days old
2 cloves of garlic
1/3 - 1/2 cup of extra virgin olive oil
8 ounces of Ricotta cheese (drained)
2 dozen gaetas (Italian olives)
8 sprigs of fresh parsley
black peppercorns

PREPARATION

1   Crush and then peel two large cloves of garlic. Using a mortar and pestle, blend and mash the garlic until it is pasty.
2   Slice away olive flesh from pits. Chop fine and blend with the garlic.
3   Add olive oil a little at a time. Continue to mash and blend all of the ingredients until smooth.
4   Chop the parsley and add to Ricotta cheese. Add freshly ground black peppercorns to taste.
5   Charcoal grill, broil or toast both sides of eight slices of Italian bread.
6   Using a knife or spatula, spread a thin layer of the olive mixture onto each slice. Dab with Ricotta cheese mixture.

VARIATIONS

Use kalamata (Greek) olives.
Use a prepared kalamata olive paste.
Add finely chopped onions or scallions after dabbing with Ricotta cheese.
Use goat cheese.

ARTICHOKE, ROASTED PEPPER AND ROMA PLUM TOMATO

*I am at the center of attention
when I am silent and let my food do the talking. . .*

INGREDIENTS

8 half inch thick slices of Italian bread, 2 - 3 days old
1 or 2 cloves of garlic
1/3 - 1/2 cup of extra virgin olive oil
2 vine ripened Roma plum tomatoes
8 artichoke hearts (Cara Mia brand)
1 twelve ounce bottle of sweet roasted red peppers (Mancini brand)
1/4 cup of grated Pecorino Romano cheese
sea salt and black peppercorns

PREPARATION

1   Slice Roma plum tomatoes very thin, lengthwise. Slice artichoke hearts, lengthwise, each into two or three pieces. Cut peppers into pieces, the width of the bread.
2   Charcoal grill, broil or toast both sides of eight slices of Italian bread.
3   Peel one or two cloves of garlic (uncrushed).
4   While the slices are still hot, rub the garlic back and forth over the entire surface, including the crust.
5   Drizzle extra virgin olive oil onto each slice, or using a pastry brush, spread the olive oil onto each slice.
6   Layer the tomatoes, followed by the artichokes and peppers.
7   Sprinkle with grated Pecorino Romano cheese.
8   Add very little sea salt and freshly ground black peppercorns to taste.
9   Broil in an oven, about four inches from the heating element until the cheese becomes lightly browned.

VARIATIONS

Use roasted green peppers.
Use Parmigiano-Reggiano or Mozzarella cheese.
Substitute another fresh tomato (squeeze lightly to remove excess juice).
Sprinkle dried oregano or basil on top.

BAKED EGGPLANT

*It is not what is done
as much as what is left undone that matters. . .*

INGREDIENTS

8 half inch thick slices of Italian bread, 2 - 3 days old
1 or 2 cloves of garlic
1/3 - 1/2 cup of extra virgin olive oil
1 large eggplant
4 tablespoons of mayonnaise
1/2 cup of bread crumbs
1/4 cup of Parmigiano-Reggiano cheese
sea salt and black peppercorns

PREPARATION

1   Cut eggplant into 16 thin, round slices. Coat both sides lightly with mayonnaise. Then coat both sides with a mixture of bread crumbs, grated Parmigiano-Reggiano cheese, sea salt and freshly ground black peppercorns. Place on a lightly greased baking sheet and bake at 350 degrees, about ten minutes per side, or until golden brown.
2   Peel one or two cloves of garlic (uncrushed).
3   Charcoal grill, broil or toast both sides of eight slices of Italian bread.
4   While the slices are still hot, rub the garlic back and forth over the entire surface, including the crust.
5   Drizzle extra virgin olive oil onto each slice, or using a pastry brush, spread the olive oil onto each slice.
6   Put two slices of baked eggplant on each slice of toast.

VARIATIONS

Use zucchini.
Use both eggplant and zucchini.
Use Pecorino Romano cheese.
Use long eggplant and slice lengthwise.
Add fresh parsley and basil to cheese and bread crumb mixture.

ROSEMARY, RED ONION AND CHILI PEPPER

Good food is not just something that happens. . .

INGREDIENTS

8 half inch thick slices of Italian bread, 2 - 3 days old
1 or 2 cloves of garlic
1/3 - 1/2 cup of extra virgin olive oil
1 small red onion (purple skinned)
1 tablespoon of fresh rosemary
1 tablespoon of dried hot, red chili pepper flakes
sea salt

PREPARATION

1   Cut onion into paper thin slices. Mince and add rosemary. Add one tablespoon of dried hot, red, chili pepper flakes. Mix well.
2   Peel one or two cloves of garlic (uncrushed).
3   Charcoal grill, broil or toast both sides of eight slices of Italian bread.
4   While the slices are still hot, rub the garlic back and forth over the entire surface, including the crust.
5   Drizzle extra virgin olive oil onto each slice, or using a pastry brush, spread the olive oil onto each slice.
6   Sprinkle sliced red onion, rosemary, and hot chili pepper flakes mixture onto each slice.
7   Add sea salt to taste.

VARIATIONS

Use Spanish onion, Maui onion, Kula onion, or Vedalia onion.
Substitute dried rosemary.

DANDELION GREENS AND PANCETTA

A blending of common sense and intuition sparks great bruschetta. . .

INGREDIENTS

8 half inch thick slices of Italian bread, 2 - 3 days old
4 cloves of garlic
1/3 - 1/2 cup of extra virgin olive oil
2 tablespoons of olive oil for frying
6 cups of dandelions (packed)
1 teaspoon of salt
4 slices of pancetta
black peppercorns

PREPARATION

1 Lightly fry pancetta (diced) in one tablespoon of olive oil until slightly browned. Remove and drain on paper toweling.
2 Wash and cut dandelions into two inch lengths.
3 Make a *soffritto*: fry two large cloves of garlic (uncrushed) in one tablespoon of olive oil on low heat until they become soft and only lightly browned, about five or six minutes. Remove from heat and let cool for five minutes. Then put the oil and garlic into a four quart pot.
4 Add one half cup of water and one teaspoon of salt.
5 Add the dandelion greens. Cook covered on medium-high until soft, about ten minutes.
6 Remove and drain the greens in a colander. Squeeze out most of the juice using the bottom of a soup bowl or a large spoon.
7 Peel one or two cloves of garlic (uncrushed).
8 Charcoal grill, broil or toast both sides of eight slices of Italian bread.
9 While the slices are still hot, rub the garlic back and forth over the entire surface, including the crust.
10 Drizzle extra virgin olive oil onto each slice, or using a pastry brush, spread the olive oil onto each slice.
11 Spread the cooked greens onto each slice. Top with chopped pancetta.
12 Add freshly ground black peppercorns to taste.

VARIATIONS

Substitute bacon. Fry crisp and drain off all fat. Drain on paper toweling.
If dandelions are unavailable, substitute escarole, spinach, endive, kale, beet leaves, or Swiss chard.

GRILLED EGGPLANT AND MOZZARELLA

Some people eat to live; others live to eat.
Find a balance. . .

INGREDIENTS

8 half inch slices of Italian bread, 2 - 3 days old
1 or 2 cloves of garlic
1/3 - 1/2 cup of extra virgin olive oil
1 large eggplant
2 tablespoons of extra virgin olive oil
8 ounces of mozzarella cheese
sea salt and black peppercorns

PREPARATION

1 Cut the eggplant lengthwise into eight slices, about a quarter inch thick.
2 Baste both sides with olive oil, sprinkle with salt and freshly ground black peppercorns, and cook on a charcoal grill for about fifteen minutes, turning several times. (Time will differ depending on the heat from the charcoal grill, a gas grill, or a stove top grill). Remove from the grill when browned, soft and scored.
3 Grate mozzarella cheese into a large bowl.
4 Peel one or two cloves of garlic.
5 Charcoal grill, broil or toast eight slices of Italian bread.
6 While the slices are still hot, rub the garlic back and forth over the entire surface, including the crust.
7 Drizzle extra virgin olive oil onto each slice, or using a pastry brush, spread the olive oil onto each slice.
8 Place one slice of eggplant onto each piece of toast. Sprinkle grated mozzarella cheese on top.
9 Arrange the toast on a large baking sheet and broil two to three minutes, about four inches from the heating element, until the mozzarella cheese melts.

VARIATIONS

Substitute jack cheese, white cheddar , or a seasoned white cheddar (e.g., sesame or caraway seeds).
Top with a colorful chopped red vegetable, such as vine ripened Roma plum tomatoes or pimiento.
Top with pitted and diced gaeta or kalamata olives.

CUCUMBER AND BALSAMIC VINEGAR

The new is in the old. . .
What one thinks of as new is often rediscovery. . .
And the old is often found in the new. . .

INGREDIENTS

8 half inch thick slices of Italian bread, 2 - 3 days old
1 or 2 cloves of garlic
1/3 - 1/2 cup of extra virgin olive oil
2 medium cucumbers
1/8 cup of balsamic vinegar
1 teaspoon of dried oregano
sea salt and black peppercorns
1 teaspoon of fresh dill

PREPARATION

1 Peel cucumbers and cut into very thin slices.
2 Place cucumbers in a large bowl. Add balsamic vinegar, oregano, sea salt and black peppercorns. Toss lightly. Marinate one hour. Drain in a colander.
3 Peel one or two cloves of garlic (uncrushed).
4 Charcoal grill, broil or toast both sides of eight slices of Italian bread.
5 While the slices are still hot, rub the garlic back and forth over the entire surface, including the crust.
6 Drizzle extra virgin olive oil onto each slice, or using a pastry brush, spread the olive oil onto each slice.
7 Layer slices of cucumber on each slice of toast. Sprinkle with fresh dill.

VARIATIONS

Use dried dill
Use dried basil.
Garnish with pitted and chopped gaetas (Italian) or kalamata (Greek) olives.
Use chopped onions or chopped scallions.

ARTICHOKE

To know, don't ask what it is. Eat it. . .

INGREDIENTS

8 half inch thick slices of Italian bread, 2 - 3 days old
2 cloves of garlic
1/3 - 1/2 cup of extra virgin olive oil
16 marinated artichoke hearts (Cara Mia brand)
1/2 cup of fresh basil
1 cup of grated Mozzarella cheese
sea salt and black peppercorns

PREPARATION

1 Drain the artichoke hearts in a colander, rinse twice, and pat dry with paper towels.
2 Crush and then peel two cloves of garlic. Using a mortar and pestle, blend and mash the garlic until it is pasty. Add the extra virgin olive oil.
3 Slice, chop, and then mince the artichoke hearts.
4 Charcoal grill, broil or toast both sides of eight slices of Italian bread.
5 While the bread is still hot, use a pastry brush to spread the garlic and olive oil mixture over the entire surface, including the crust.
6 Spread the minced artichoke hearts evenly onto each slice.
7 Add sea salt and freshly ground black peppercorns to taste.
8 Sprinkle each slice with grated Mozzarella cheese.
9 Arrange the slices on an ungreased baking sheet. Broil in an oven, about four inches from the heating element, until the Mozzarella cheese melts and becomes lightly browned.

VARIATIONS

Use Fontina, Fontinella, jack or white cheddar cheese.
Use a 1.6 ounce jar of ready made caraciofina sanremo (prepared artichoke paste).
Add chopped vine ripened Roma plum tomatoes.
Use dried basil.

SHALLOTS AND TOMATO

If you truly wish to understand others,
start first by seeking an understanding of the foods they eat. . .

INGREDIENTS

8 half inch thick slices of Italian bread, 2 - 3 days old
1 or 2 cloves of garlic
1/3 - 1/2 cup of extra virgin olive oil
2 large vine ripened Roma plum tomatoes
2 shallots
1/8 cup of balsamic vinegar
4 ounces of Mozzarella cheese
sea salt and black peppercorns

PREPARATION

1 Dice the Roma plum tomatoes and shallots. Mix in a bowl with balsamic vinegar, sea salt and freshly ground black peppercorns, to taste. Allow to marinate one hour.
2 Peel one or two cloves of garlic (uncrushed).
3 Charcoal grill, broil or toast both sides of eight slices of Italian bread.
4 While the slices are still hot, rub the garlic back and forth over the entire surface, including the crust.
5 Drizzle extra virgin olive oil onto each slice, or using a pastry brush, spread the olive oil onto each slice.
6 Drain the tomato and shallot mixture in a colander. Lightly press to remove some of the juices.
7 Spoon the tomato and shallot mixture onto each slice. Sprinkle with grated Mozzarella cheese.

VARIATIONS

Use Parmigiano-Reggiano cheese.
Substitute another fresh tomato (squeeze lightly to remove excess juice).
Substitute scallions for shallots.
Sprinkle with dried oregano or basil.

OLIVE

An olive needs light to grow, salt brine and darkness to ripen,
and our palates to appreciate...

INGREDIENTS

8 half inch thick slices of Italian bread, 2 - 3 days old
2 large cloves of garlic
1/3 - 1/2 cup of extra virgin olive oil
2 dozen gaetas (Italian) or kalamata (Greek) olives
2 tablespoons of fresh oregano
1/4 cup of grated Pecorino Romano cheese
black peppercorns

PREPARATION

1 Crush and then peel two large cloves of garlic.
2 Using a mortar and pestle, blend and mash the garlic until it is pasty.
3 Slice away the olive flesh from the pits. Chop fine, add to the garlic paste, and blend well.
4 Add olive oil a little at a time. Continue to mash and blend the ingredients until smooth.
5 Blend in the oregano, grated Pecorino Romano cheese, and freshly ground black peppercorns
   to taste.
6 Place the mixture in a small pot and heat it until it becomes slightly warmed. Stir frequently.
7 Charcoal grill, broil or toast both sides of eight slices of Italian bread.
8 While the bread is still hot, spread the warmed mixture over the entire surface, including the crust.

VARIATIONS

Use Parmigiano-Reggiano cheese.
Use dried oregano.
Use large green olives (cerignola) or Sicilian style green olives.
Spread the olive mixture onto slices at room temperature.

CHICKEN LIVER PÂTÉ

No expectations. . . no disappointments. . .

INGREDIENTS

8 half inch thick slices of Italian bread, 2 - 3 days old
1 or 2 cloves of garlic
1/3 - 1/2 cup of extra virgin olive oil
1 small onion
1 small stalk of celery
sea salt and black peppercorns
6 chicken livers
1/2 cup chicken broth
1/4 cup fresh parsley

PREPARATION

1 Dice the onion and celery and add to one quart of boiling water. Add sea salt and freshly ground peppercorns to taste. Add chicken livers. Cook for fifteen minutes.
2 Drain the cooked chicken livers and then blend in a food processor until smooth. Add some of the chicken broth a little at a time, but only as much as needed to keep the mixture moist and pasty.
3 Peel one or two cloves of garlic (uncrushed).
4 Charcoal grill, broil or toast both sides of eight slices of Italian bread.
5 While the slices are still hot, rub the garlic back and forth over the entire surface, including the crust.
6 Drizzle extra virgin olive oil onto each slice, or using a pastry brush, spread the olive oil onto each slice.
7 With a knife or spatula, spread each slice with a thin layer of pâté.
8 Sprinkle with finely chopped parsley.

VARIATIONS

Substitute goose liver or turkey liver.

SPINACH AND EGG

A cook doesn't complete a recipe
until the food is consumed. . .

INGREDIENTS

8 half inch thick slices of Italian bread, 2 - 3 days old
1 or 2 cloves of garlic
1/3 - 1/2 cup of extra virgin olive oil
3 large eggs
1 very large bunch of spinach
sea salt and black peppercorns

PREPARATION

1 Hard boil three large eggs. Shell and cut into quarter inch slices.
2 Wash the spinach and chop (coarse). Put in a Pyrex dish with one third cup of water and cover with plastic wrap. Microwave for three minutes. Time may vary depending on the power and setting of the microwave.
3 Remove spinach. Drain well in a colander.
4 Peel one or two cloves of garlic (uncrushed).
5 Charcoal grill, broil or toast both sides of eight slices of Italian bread.
6 While the slices are still hot, rub the garlic back and forth over the entire surface, including the crust.
7 Drizzle extra virgin olive oil onto each slice, or using a pastry brush, spread the olive oil onto each slice.
8 Spoon the spinach onto each slice and top with slices of hard boiled egg.
9 Drizzle more extra virgin oil onto the egg and spinach.
10 Add sea salt and freshly ground black peppercorns to taste.

VARIATIONS

Use any other greens in season, such as escarole, mustard greens, endive, kale, beet leaves, or Swiss chard. If fresh vegetables are unavailable, substitute frozen spinach (thaw, warm, drain well and squeeze out the juice).

FRIED POLENTA SANS TOAST

All that we give to others comes back into our own lives. . .

INGREDIENTS

1 cup of yellow corn meal
1/2 teaspoon of salt
2 large cloves of garlic
1/2 cup grated Pecorino Romano cheese
1 tablespoon of olive oil
1/4 cup of flour
2 large eggs

1/2 cup of bread crumbs
1/3 cup of fresh basil
1/2 cup of fresh parsley
black peppercorns
1/3 cup of light olive oil for frying
1 cup of marinara sauce
   (home made or prepared)

PREPARATION

1 To prepare the polenta, boil three cups of water. Add salt. Lower to medium heat and add the cornmeal a little at a time, stirring constantly. Cook for six minutes, stirring constantly to avoid lumping and sticking.

2 Add two large cloves of garlic (finely minced) and one quarter cup of grated Pecorino Romano cheese. Blend in well. Cook for another two minutes, stirring constantly.

3 Ladle the cooked polenta into an eight inch Pyrex dish coated with olive oil. Spread and smooth the top of the polenta with a spatula. Add one teaspoon of olive oil to the top and continue to smooth out. Cover and refrigerate two hours to cool and solidify.

4 Remove the polenta from the refrigerator. Turn it out onto a lightly floured cutting board. Slice into eight pieces. Dust with more flour.

5 Dip pieces into well-beaten eggs and then coat in a mixture of bread crumbs, grated Pecorino Romano cheese, chopped basil and parsley, and freshly ground peppercorns to taste. Press the mixture onto polenta well.

6 Fry four pieces at a time in a twelve inch nonstick frying pan in one third cup of light olive oil. Fry each side until golden brown. Remove and spoon warmed marinara sauce onto each slice.

VARIATIONS

Substitute grated Parmigiano-Reggiano cheese.

THREE PEPPERCORNS

Small things carry significant meaning.
Think bruschetta!

INGREDIENTS

8 half inch thick slices of Italian bread, 2 - 3 days old
2 cloves of garlic
1/3 - 1/2 cup of extra virgin olive oil
12 black peppercorns
8 red peppercorns
4 green peppercorns
sea salt

PREPARATION

1 Crush and then peel two cloves of garlic. Using a mortar and pestle, blend and mash the garlic until it is pasty. Add the olive oil.
2 Using a mallet and chopping board, smash each peppercorn and blend with the garlic and olive oil mixture.
3 Charcoal grill, broil or toast both sides of eight slices of Italian bread.
4 While the bread is still hot, use a pastry brush to spread the peppercorn, garlic and olive oil mixture over the entire surface, including the crust.
5 Sprinkle each slice with grated Pecorino Romano cheese.
6 Add very little sea salt.

VARIATIONS

Use only red, green or black peppercorns.
Use Parmigiano-Reggiano cheese.
Omit sea salt.

EGG AND CHEESE

Do less. . . and more will result. . .

INGREDIENTS

8 half inch thick slices of Italian bread, 2 - 3 days old
3 cloves of garlic
1/3 - 1/2 cup of extra virgin olive oil
4 leaves of fresh basil
2 sprigs of fresh parsley
3 large eggs
1/4 cup of grated Asiago cheese
1/4 cup of bread crumbs
1 whole sweet red roasted pepper (Mancini brand)
sea salt and black peppercorns

PREPARATION

1 Break three eggs into a large bowl. Beat lightly.
2 Chop fine one clove of garlic, basil and parsley. Add to the eggs and mix in well.
3 Blend in the grated Asiago cheese, bread crumbs, sea salt and freshly ground peppercorns, to taste. Mix with a fork for about one minute.
4 Peel one or two cloves of garlic (uncrushed).
5 Charcoal grill, broil or toast both sides of eight slices of Italian bread.
6 While the slices are still hot, rub the garlic back and forth over the entire surface, including the crust.
7 Drizzle extra virgin olive oil onto each slice, or using a pastry brush, spread the olive oil onto each slice.
8 Arrange slices of Italian bread, grilled, broiled or toasted on both sides, on an ungreased baking sheet.
9 With a knife or spatula, spread the egg mixture evenly onto each slice.
10 Top each slice (diagonally) with three or four thinly sliced strips of roasted red pepper.
11 Broil in an oven, about four inches from the heating element until the egg solidifies and becomes lightly browned.

VARIATIONS

Use Pecorino Romano or Parmigiano-Reggiano cheese.

MARINATED EGGPLANT

Do not be saddened by black clouds cradling drenching rains...
Think instead of those who dance in joyous celebration
at its drifting life force that brings sustenance to our tables...

INGREDIENTS

8 half inch thick slices of Italian bread, 2 - 3 days old
3 cloves of garlic
1/3 - 1/2 cup of extra virgin olive oil
1/4 cup cider vinegar
1 large round eggplant
1/4 cup of extra virgin olive oil

1 stalk of celery
1/2 medium onion
1 medium green bell pepper
2 tablespoons fresh parsley
1 teaspoon fresh oregano
sea salt and black peppercorns

PREPARATION

1 Bring eight cups of water to a boil. Add one eighth cup of cider vinegar.
2 Slice the eggplant into round pieces one inch thick. Put the pieces into water and vinegar and cook until soft.
3 Remove to a colander. Drain well and refrigerate.
4 After the eggplant has cooled, add one eighth cup of cider vinegar, one quarter cup of extra virgin olive oil, and chopped celery, onion, green pepper, one clove of garlic, and parsley. Add oregano, finely ground sea salt and freshly ground peppercorns. Mix all ingredients, cover, and refrigerate overnight.
5 Remove the eggplant from the refrigerator and uncover it. Allow it to stand until it reaches room temperature. Mix well.
6 Peel one or two cloves of garlic (uncrushed).
7 Charcoal grill, broil or toast both sides of eight slices of Italian bread.
8 While the slices are still hot, rub the garlic back and forth over the entire surface, including the crust.
9 Drizzle extra virgin olive oil onto each slice, or using a pastry brush, spread the olive oil onto each slice.
10 Spoon generous amounts of the eggplant mixture onto each slice.

VARIATIONS

Substitute balsamic vinegar.
Add one carrot, chopped fine.
Use hot chili pepper.
Use dried basil and oregano.

GREEN TOMATO

*Nothing that has happened to you
has not happened to me. . .*

INGREDIENTS

8 half inch thick slices of Italian bread, 2 - 3 days old
3 cloves of garlic
1/3 - 1/2 cup of extra virgin olive oil
4 medium green tomatoes
1/4 cup of extra virgin olive oil
2 teaspoons of dried oregano
1 large clove of garlic
sea salt and black peppercorns

PREPARATION

1 Slice green tomatoes very thin, about one-eighth of an inch. Place them in a large dish or bowl and add a mixture of one quarter cup of extra virgin olive oil, oregano, one large clove of garlic (minced), sea salt and freshly ground peppercorns to taste. Toss lightly, making sure both sides of tomato slices are coated well.
2 Layer the slices of tomato in a flat-bottomed bowl or crock. Cover and refrigerate for two days.
3 Remove the tomatoes from the refrigerator. Toss lightly. Allow them to stand until they reach room temperature.
4 Peel one or two cloves of garlic (uncrushed).
5 Charcoal grill, broil or toast both sides of eight slices of Italian bread.
6 While the slices are still hot, rub the garlic back and forth over the entire surface, including the crust.
7 Drizzle extra virgin olive oil onto each slice, or using a pastry brush, spread the olive oil onto each slice.
8 Layer green tomatoes onto each slice of toast.

VARIATIONS

Use semi-ripe tomatoes.

ASPARAGUS

Routine destroys what could be great food. . .

INGREDIENTS

8 half inch thick slices of Italian bread, 2 - 3 days old
1 or 2 cloves of garlic
1/3 - 1/2 cup of extra virgin olive oil
1 large bunch of asparagus (24 spears)
2 tablespoons of extra virgin olive oil
sea salt and black peppercorns

PREPARATION

1 Cut off the bottom quarter of asparagus spears. Wash and drain. Place the asparagus in a Pyrex dish. Add one third cup of water, cover with plastic wrap, and microwave on high for seven minutes. Time may vary depending on the power and setting of the microwave. Remove and drain the liquid.
2 Peel one or two cloves of garlic (uncrushed).
3 Charcoal grill, broil or toast both sides of eight slices of Italian bread.
4 While the slices are still hot, rub the garlic back and forth over the entire surface, including the crust.
5 Drizzle extra virgin olive oil onto each slice, or using a pastry brush, spread the olive oil onto each slice.
6 Place asparagus spears on bread, alternating direction of tips.
7 Very lightly drizzle two tablespoons of extra virgin olive oil onto the spears.
8 Add sea salt and freshly ground black peppercorns to taste.

VARIATIONS

Sprinkle with Parmigiano-Reggiano cheese.
Instead of drizzling extra virgin olive oil on top, lightly drizzle freshly squeezed lemon juice.
After microwaving the asparagus, put the spears into a food processor. Add two tablespoons of olive oil. Blend until smooth, but with small pieces of asparagus still visible. Remove and mix with two tablespoons of Parmigiano-Reggiano cheese. Spread onto bread after step 5. Skip steps 6 and 7.

FAVA

Although we look at the same foods,
they do not always carry the same meaning.

INGREDIENTS

8 half inch thick slices of Italian bread, 2 - 3 days old
1 or 2 cloves of garlic
1/3 - 1/2 cup of extra virgin olive oil
4 dozen fava
1/2 onion
1 tablespoon of olive oil for frying
1/4 pound of pancetta
sea salt and peppercorns

PREPARATION

1   Shell the fava. Bring two cups of water to a boil and add the fava, sea salt and freshly ground peppercorns to taste. Cook on medium heat until soft. Drain in a colander.
2   Dice the onion and pancetta.
3   In a six inch skillet, fry the onion in one tablespoon of olive oil until lightly browned. Add pancetta and fry another two minutes. Combine the fava beans, onions and pancetta. Mix well and cook another two minutes.
4   Peel one or two cloves of garlic (uncrushed).
5   Charcoal grill, broil or toast both sides of eight slices of Italian bread.
6   While the slices are still hot, rub the garlic back and forth over the entire surface, including the crust.
7   Drizzle extra virgin olive oil onto each slice, or using a pastry brush, spread the olive oil onto each slice.
8   Spoon the fava bean mixture onto each slice of toast.

VARIATIONS

Substitute one twelve ounce jar of prepared fava beans if fresh fava beans are not in season. Drain the liquid.
Use lima beans.
Substitute diced bacon for pancetta. Place the crispy fried or broiled bacon on paper toweling to absorb the fat.

FRIED ONIONS AND GREEN PEPPERS

*The joy of cooking occurs
when you watch the faces of those who savor your bruschetta!*

INGREDIENTS

8 half inch thick slices of Italian bread, 2 - 3 days old
2 cloves of garlic
1/3 - 1/2 cup of extra virgin olive oil
1 large onion
3 green bell peppers
2 tablespoons of olive oil
sea salt

PREPARATION

1 Peel and slice the onion. Wash and then core the green peppers. Slice them into pieces about one quarter of an inch thick. Dry well with paper toweling.
2 Fry the onions and green peppers in a skillet in two tablespoons of olive oil until soft and lightly browned. Turn frequently.
3 Peel two cloves of garlic.
4 Charcoal grill, broil or toast both sides of eight slices of Italian bread.
5 While the slices are still hot, rub the garlic back and forth over the entire surface, including the crust.
6 Drizzle extra virgin olive oil onto each slice, or using a pastry brush, spread the olive oil onto each slice.
7 Spoon the onions and peppers onto each slice of toast.
8 Add sea salt to taste.

VARIATIONS

Use hot green chili peppers.
Use a variety of bell peppers (green, red, yellow, purple, white).

BONE MARROW

The soul of food is frequently found in its center...

INGREDIENTS

8 half inch thick slices of Italian bread, 2 - 3 days old
3 cloves of garlic
1/3 - 1/2 cup of extra virgin olive oil
8 to 10 large soup bones (e.g., shank)
1 medium onion
2 stalks of celery
2 medium carrots
4 sprigs of fresh Italian parsley
6 fresh basil leaves
1/2 teaspoon of sea salt
1 fourteen ounce can of whole tomatoes
sea salt and black peppercorns

PREPARATION

1 Bring two quarts of water to a boil. Add the soup bones, minced onion, one large clove of garlic (crushed), chopped celery and carrots, finely chopped parsley and basil, and one half teaspoon of sea salt.
2 Drain the liquid from the whole tomatoes and squash the tomatoes well. Drain any remaining liquid and then add the tomatoes to the pot. Cover and cook on medium heat for an hour and a half.
3 Remove the soup bones and cool. Scoop the marrow into a bowl. Drain any liquid and mash the marrow with a fork. Strain and refrigerate the stock for future use.
4 Peel one or two cloves of garlic.
5 Charcoal grill, broil or toast both sides of eight slices of Italian bread.
6 While the slices are still hot, rub the garlic back and forth over the entire surface, including the crust.
7 Drizzle extra virgin olive oil onto each slice, or using a pastry brush, spread the olive oil onto each slice. (Reduce the amount of olive oil considerably if the marrow is very oily).
8 With a knife or spatula, spread a thin layer of the marrow onto each slice.
9 Add sea salt and freshly ground peppercorns to taste.

VARIATIONS

Sprinkle with grated Asiago cheese (omit sea salt).

SARDINES AND LEMON

Empty the mind. . . still the body . . .
Open the heart. . . excite the palate. . .

INGREDIENTS

8 half inch thick slices of Italian bread, 2 - 3 days old
1 or 2 cloves of garlic
1/3 - 1/2 cup of extra virgin olive oil
2 four ounce cans of sardines (packed in water or soy)
1 tablespoon of cider vinegar
2 tablespoons of extra virgin olive oil
1/2 teaspoon of salt
1 lemon
black peppercorns

PREPARATION

1 Drain the liquid from the sardines. Cut into one inch pieces.
2 Add vinegar and two tablespoons of extra virgin olive oil. Mix well.
3 Add one half teaspoon of salt, the juice of half a lemon, and freshly ground black peppercorns
   to taste. Add paper thin slices of the remaining half lemon. Remove any seeds. Mix well and
   refrigerate. Stir occasionally.
4 Peel one or two cloves of garlic (uncrushed).
5 Charcoal grill, broil or toast both sides of eight slices of Italian bread.
6 While the slices are still hot, rub the garlic back and forth over the entire surface, including the crust.
7 Drizzle extra virgin olive oil onto each slice, or using a pastry brush, spread the olive oil onto each
   slice.
8 Remove the sardine mixture from the refrigerator one hour before use in order to bring it to room
   temperature. Spoon the sardine mixture onto each slice.

VARIATIONS

Substitute balsamic vinegar.
Substitute tangerines. Remove seeds.

DROWNED BRUSCHETTA

"Saving" the drowned bruschetta brings joy to the palate. . .

INGREDIENTS

8 half inch thick slices of Italian bread, 2 - 3 days old
1 or 2 cloves of garlic
1/3 - 1/2 cup of extra virgin olive oil
sea salt
2 small chicken breasts
1 carrot
1 small onion
2 stalks of celery
salt and black peppercorns
4 or 5 sprigs of fresh parsley
1/4 cup of Pecorino Romano cheese, grated

PREPARATION

1 Fill a four-quart pot two-thirds with water and bring to a boil. Turn heat down to medium and add chicken breasts, chopped carrot, onion, and celery. Season with salt, freshly ground black peppercorns to taste, and parsley. Cook one hour.
2 Strain the soup into another pot and place it on the stove to keep it hot. Refrigerate the chicken and vegetables for future use.
3 Peel one or two cloves of garlic.
4 Charcoal grill, broil or toast eight slices of Italian bread.
5 While the slices are still hot, rub the garlic back and forth over the entire surface, including the crust.
6 Drizzle extra virgin olive oil onto each slice, or using a pastry brush, spread the olive oil onto each slice.
7 Using a grinder, sprinkle sea salt to taste on each slice. (optional)
8 Place one slice of bruschetta, more if small, into soup bowls. Ladle chicken soup broth around the bruschetta, enough to cover it. Sprinkle with grated Pecorino Romano cheese and garnish with a spring of fresh parsley and a few fresh leaves of basil.

VARIATIONS

Use grated Parmigiano-Reggiano cheese.
Instead of using whole slices of bruschetta, cut them into bite-sized pieces.

FRIED CARDOON

The simplest of foods delights the palate and elevates the soul.

INGREDIENTS

8 half inch thick slices of Italian bread, 2 - 3 days old
1 or 2 cloves of garlic
1/3 - 1/2 cup of extra virgin olive oil
1 large bunch of cardoon
1/2 cup of bread crumbs
1/2 cup of Pecorino Romano cheese
1 tablespoon of dried parsley
1 tablespoon of dried basil
2 large eggs
1 cup of light olive oil for frying
sea salt and black peppercorns

PREPARATION

1 Remove and discard cardoon leaves. Wash and trim the cardoon stems and peel the thin skin with a knife or peeler. Place them in a steamer and cook until tender.
2 Mix the bread crumbs, cheese, parsley, basil and salt and freshly ground peppercorns to taste.
3 Beat two eggs well with a fork.
4 Heat one cup of light olive oil in an electric skillet or deep fry.
5 Dip each cardoon in egg and then in the bread crumb, cheese and spice mixture.
6 Drop into oil, fry until golden brown, and remove them to paper toweling to drain.
7 Peel one or two cloves of garlic.
8 Charcoal grill, broil or toast both sides of eight slices of Italian bread.
9 While the slices are still hot, rub the garlic back and forth over the entire surface, including the crust.
10 Drizzle extra virgin olive oil onto each slice, or using a pastry brush, spread the olive oil onto each slice.
11 Place the fried cardoon lengthwise on the toast.

VARIATIONS

Sprinkle with more Romano Pecorino cheese.
Substitute asparagus.

TOMATO, ANCHOVY AND SCALLIONS

It is not just the food on the platter that makes it pleasing to the eye. . .
It is also the spatial arrangement. . .

INGREDIENTS

8 half inch thick slices of Italian bread, 2 - 3 days old
1 or 2 cloves of garlic
1/3 - 1/2 cup of extra virgin olive oil
2 large vine ripened Roma plum tomatoes
1 two ounce can of anchovy fillets
1 bunch of scallions
black peppercorns

PREPARATION

1   Peel one or two cloves of garlic.
2   Charcoal grill, broil or toast both sides of eight slices of Italian bread.
3   While the slices are still hot, rub the garlic back and forth over the entire surface, including the crust.
4   Drizzle extra virgin olive oil onto each slice, or using a pastry brush, spread the olive oil onto each slice.
5   Add thinly sliced Roma plum tomatoes, two or three anchovies (drained well), and a sprinkling of chopped scallions on each slice.
6   Add freshly ground black peppercorns to taste.

VARIATIONS

Use chives or onions.
Use the oil from the anchovies and reduce the amount of extra virgin olive oil.

BROCCOLINI

It also takes darkness for a flower to grow. . .

INGREDIENTS

8 half inch slices of Italian bread, 2 - 3 days old
4 cloves of garlic
1/3 - 1/2 cup of extra virgin olive oil
2 bunches of broccolini (equivalent to 8 cups, packed)
2 tablespoons of olive oil for frying
1/4 cup of water
1/2 teaspoon of salt
sea salt and black peppercorns

PREPARATION

1 Make a *soffritto*: fry two cloves of garlic (uncrushed) in two tablespoons of olive oil. Fry on low heat until the garlic becomes soft and only lightly browned, about five or six minutes. Cool and then add one quarter cup of water and one half teaspoon of salt.

2 Wash and cut the broccolini into four inch lengths. Add to the *soffritto*. Cook covered for fifteen minutes on medium heat or until the broccolini turns a bright green. Remove to a colander and drain well.

3 Peel one or two cloves of garlic.

4 Charcoal grill, broil or toast eight slices of Italian bread.

5 While the slices are still hot, rub the garlic back and forth over the entire surface, including the crust.

6 Drizzle extra virgin olive oil onto each slice, or using a pastry brush, spread the olive oil onto each slice.

7 Spoon the cooked broccolini onto each slice.

8 Sprinkle sea salt and freshly ground black peppercorns to taste.

VARIATIONS

Use broccoli.

FINOCCHIO AND PIMIENTO

*When you cook, stop thinking too much. . .
and start feeling. . .*

INGREDIENTS

8 half inch thick slices of Italian bread, 2 - 3 days old
1 or 2 cloves of garlic
1/3 - 1/2 cup of extra virgin olive oil
1 large finocchio (fennel)
1 tablespoon of extra virgin olive oil
1/2 cup pimiento
1/2 cup grated Asiago cheese
1/3 cup bread crumbs
black peppercorns
sea salt

PREPARATION

1 Remove the tops from the finocchio. Cut lengthwise into sixteen pieces, first by quartering and then by quartering once again. Wash the finnochio. Drain and pat dry with paper toweling.
2 Coat the finnochio stalks with one tablespoon of extra virgin olive oil and place in a Pyrex dish. Cover with plastic wrap and microwave until soft.
3 Remove the plastic wrap and sprinkle with grated Asiago cheese, diced pimiento, bread crumbs, freshly ground black peppercorns, and sea salt to taste. Place under a broiler and brown lightly.
4 Peel one or two cloves of garlic.
5 Charcoal grill, broil or toast both sides of eight slices of Italian bread.
6 While the slices are still hot, rub the garlic back and forth over the entire surface, including the crust.
7 Drizzle extra virgin olive oil onto each slice, or using a pastry brush, spread the olive oil onto each slice.
8 Place two pieces of finocchio on each slice.

VARIATIONS

Steam the finocchio pieces, cut, and then mash them. Squeeze out liquid. Combine with pimiento, olive oil, and salt. Spread onto the toast.

BEANS AND GREENS

It is not only the end that is important.
It is also the path to that end.

INGREDIENTS

8 half inch thick slices of Italian bread, 2 - 3 days old
4 cloves of garlic
1/3 - 1/2 cup of extra virgin olive oil
1 medium sized smoked ham hock
1 medium onion
1 tablespoon of olive oil

1 fourteen ounce can of prepared baby lima beans
6 cups of dandelions or greens in season (spinach, Swiss chard, endive, beet greens, mustard greens, escarole, turnip greens)
black peppercorns

PREPARATION

1 Bring six cups of water to a boil. Add two cloves of garlic and the ham hock. Cook on medium heat for one hour. Remove to a colander. Save the liquid. Discard the fat around the ham hock. Break up the remaining meat with a fork and return to liquid.
2 Slice and fry the onions in one tablespoon of olive oil until soft and browned lightly.
3 Drain off the liquid from lima beans.
4 Add the fried onions, lima beans, and freshly ground black peppercorns, to taste, to the ham hock and its liquid. Cook for one half hour on medium heat.
5 Wash the greens and drain. Cut into three inch lengths. Add the greens and cook another half hour.
6 Remove two cups (or more if needed) of the beans and greens to a colander. Press lightly to remove most of the juice.
7 Peel one or two cloves of garlic.
8 Charcoal grill, broil or toast both sides of eight slices of Italian bread.
9 While the slices are still hot, rub the garlic back and forth over the entire surface, including the crust.
10 Drizzle extra virgin olive oil onto each slice, or using a pastry brush, spread the olive oil onto each slice.
11 Spoon slightly cooled beans and greens onto each slice.

VARIATIONS

Use large lima beans.
Substitute fava beans.
Top with grated Pecorino Romano cheese.

FRIED MOZZARELLA

When we all partake of the same food, we become one. . .

INGREDIENTS

8 half inch thick slices of Italian bread, 2 - 3 days old
1 or 2 cloves of garlic
1/3 - 1/2 cup of extra virgin olive oil
1 pound of Mozzarella cheese
2 large eggs
1/3 cup flour
1/3 cup of seasoned bread crumbs (Progresso brand)
1 cup olive oil (for frying)
black peppercorns

PREPARATION

1   Cut Mozzarella cheese into pieces about three inches long and one quarter inch thick.
2   Heat olive oil in a deep fryer or electric skillet.
3   Dip slices of Mozzarella in flour, then egg, and then in seasoned bread crumbs. Fry until golden brown. Remove and drain on paper towing.
4   Peel one or two large cloves of garlic.
5   Charcoal grill, broil or toast both sides of eight slices of Italian bread.
6   While the slices are still hot, rub the garlic back and forth over the entire surface, including the crust.
7   Drizzle extra virgin olive oil onto each slice, or using a pastry brush, spread the olive oil onto each slice.
8   Add fried Mozzarella. Sprinkle on freshly ground peppercorns to taste.

VARIATIONS

Substitute Provolone cheese.
Use red chili pepper flakes.
Make seasoned bread crumbs by adding dried parsley, dried basil, dried oregano, salt and pepper.

ROMA PLUM TOMATO RUB

The tomato came from the America's, and the Italians liberated it!

INGREDIENTS

8 half inch thick slices of Italian bread, 2 - 3 days old
1 or 2 cloves of garlic
1/3 - 1/2 cup of extra virgin olive oil
1 large vine ripened Roma plum tomato
2 teaspoons of fresh oregano
sea salt and black peppercorns

PREPARATION

1   Cut the Roma plum tomato in half.
2   Peel one or two cloves of garlic (uncrushed).
3   Charcoal grill, broil or toast both sides of eight slices of Italian bread.
4   While the slices are still hot, rub the garlic back and forth over the entire surface, including the crust.
5   Drizzle extra virgin olive oil onto each slice, or using a pastry brush, spread the olive oil onto each slice.
6   Rub the cut side of the tomato back and forth over the entire surface, including the crust.
7   Sprinkle with fresh oregano.
8   Sprinkle sea salt and fresh ground peppercorns to taste.

VARIATIONS

Substitute another kind of tomato in season.
Use green tomatoes for the rub.
Top with chopped onions.
Use dried oregano.
Sprinkle with grated Parmigiano-Reggiano cheese.

CHESTNUT

Food to some may be viewed as nourishment alone,
but to be complete,
it should also lift the spirit. . .

INGREDIENTS

8 half inch slices of Italian bread, 2 - 3 days old
1/3 - 1/2 cup of extra virgin olive oil
1 or 2 cloves of garlic
3 dozen chestnuts (or one 8.75 ounce can of prepared chestnut spread)

PREPARATION

1   With a sharp pointed knife, make three or four slits into each chestnut. Bring a quart of water to a boil. Add the chestnuts and cook on medium heat until tender. Test doneness by piercing a few of the chestnuts with a toothpick. Remove and rinse the chestnuts in cold water. Allow to cool, and then peel off the skins.
2   Chop the chestnuts very fine. Using a mortar and pestle, mash the chestnuts until they become slightly creamy.
3   Peel one or two cloves of garlic.
4   Charcoal grill, broil or toast eight slices of Italian bread.
5   While the slices are still hot, rub the garlic back and forth over the entire surface, including the crust.
6   Drizzle extra virgin olive oil onto each slice, or using a pastry brush, spread the olive oil onto each slice.
7   Spoon the chestnut paste onto each slice and spread with a knife.
8   Sprinkle lightly with nutmeg.

VARIATIONS

Sprinkle with paprika.
Substitute walnuts.
Sprinkle with freshly chopped basil.

CAPONATA

*Food never tastes as good
as when you are sharing it in the company of others. . .*

INGREDIENTS

8 half inch thick slices of Italian bread
4 cloves of garlic
1/3 - 1/2 cup of extra virgin olive oil
2 medium or 1 large eggplant
Salt and black peppercorns to taste
6 Italian black olives (gaeta or kalamata)
6 large green olives (cerignola)
8 vine ripened Roma plum tomatoes

1 small onion
1 stalk of celery
2 tablespoons of pine nuts
1 tablespoon of capers
4 tablespoons of balsamic vinegar
1 teaspoon of sugar
1/2 cup of light olive oil for frying

PREPARATION

1 Slice the eggplant into quarters and then into pieces about one inch thick. Add salt and freshly ground black peppercorns to taste and let stand for forty-five minutes.
2 Heat one half cup of light olive oil in a large skillet on medium-high and fry the eggplant until soft, about ten minutes.
3 In a large bowl, mix together gaeta and cerignola olives. Remove the flesh from the pits and chop (coarse). Add Roma plum tomatoes, peeled, quartered and then halved; the onions and celery, chopped fine; two cloves of garlic, minced; pine nuts, lightly chopped; capers, drained well; balsamic vinegar and sugar. Add to the eggplant and cook on medium heat for twenty minutes, or until the mixture becomes soft. Stir frequently.
4 Peel one or two cloves of garlic.
5 Charcoal grill, broil or toast eight slices of Italian bread.
6 While the slices are still hot, rub the garlic back and forth over the entire surface, including the crust.
7 Drizzle extra virgin olive oil onto each slice, or using a pastry brush, spread the olive oil onto each slice.
8 Spoon generous amounts of the caponata, either warm or at room temperature, onto each slice.

VARIATIONS

Lightly sprinkle grated Pecorino Romano cheese on top of each slice.
Add to recipe one half bell pepper (coarsely chopped), and a small bottle (Mancini brand) roasted, sweet red peppers (cut into one inch pieces).

ARUGULA AND PLUM TOMATO

Arugula is green,
Italian bread is white,
Roma plum tomatoes are red.
Ah! Bruschetta con aglio—the colors of Italy's flag!

INGREDIENTS

8 half inch thick slices of Italian bread, 2 - 3 days old
4 cloves of garlic
1/3 - 1/2 cup of extra virgin olive oil
1 tablespoon of olive oil for frying
1 bunch of fresh arugula
3-4 vine ripened Roma plum tomatoes
sea salt and black peppercorns

PREPARATION

1 Slice the tomatoes into small cubes.
2 Make a *soffritto*: fry two cloves of garlic (uncrushed) in one tablespoon of olive oil. Fry on low heat until the garlic becomes soft and only lightly browned, about five or six minutes.
3 Wash the arugula and drain well. Tear the leaves into small pieces and discard the bottom stems. Cube the Roma plum tomatoes. Add both to the cooled *soffritto* and toss lightly.
4 Peel one or two large cloves of garlic.
5 Charcoal grill, broil or toast eight slices of Italian bread.
6 While the slices are still hot, rub the garlic back and forth over the entire surface, including the crust.
7 Drizzle extra virgin olive oil onto each slice, or using a pastry brush, spread the olive oil onto each slice.
8 Spoon the tomato and arugula mixture onto the toast.
9 Sprinkle sea salt and freshly ground black peppercorns to taste.

VARIATIONS

Lightly sprinkle grated Pecorino Romano cheese on top of each slice (reduce or omit salt).
Substitute other greens in season, such as endive or escarole.
Use green or half-ripe tomatoes.

BUTTERNUT SQUASH, PINE NUTS AND BACON

Food is not something you give. . .
It is something you share.

INGREDIENTS

8 half inch thick slices of Italian bread, 2 - 3 days old
1 or 2 cloves of garlic
1/3 - 1/2 cup of extra virgin olive oil
1 large butternut squash
1/2 cup pine nuts
3 vine ripened Roma plum tomatoes
1/2 pound of bacon
sea salt and black peppercorns

PREPARATION

1 Toast the pine nuts in a pan under a broiler until lightly browned. Toss the nuts periodically to toast them evenly. Time will vary.
2 Slice the bacon into one half inch pieces and fry until crisp and golden brown. Remove and drain on paper toweling.
3 Cut the butternut squash in half and remove the seeds. Place them cut side down in a Pyrex dish, cover tightly with plastic wrap, and cook for fifteen minutes (time will vary depending on size of squash and microwave power). Test for doneness with a fork.
4 Remove the squash and scoop out the pulp. Mash it with a fork until smooth.
5 Peel one or two cloves of garlic (uncrushed).
6 Charcoal grill, broil or toast both sides of eight slices of Italian bread.
7 While the slices are still hot, rub the garlic back and forth over the entire surface, including the crust.
8 Drizzle extra virgin olive oil onto each slice, or using a pastry brush, spread the olive oil onto each slice.
9 Spread the butternut squash onto each slice of toast and sprinkle on toasted pine nuts and bacon.

VARIATIONS

Use spaghetti squash or acorn squash.
Sprinkle with nutmeg.

GRILLED VEGETABLES

A colorful medley of grilled vegetables is al fresco at its best!

INGREDIENTS

8 half inch thick slices of Italian bread,
  2 - 3 days old
1 or 2 cloves of garlic
1/3 - 1/2 cup of extra virgin olive oil
4 vine ripened Roma plum tomatoes
sea salt
1 green bell pepper
1 red bell pepper
1 small eggplant
16 leaves of long radicchio

1 large onion
1 yellow zucchini
1 green zucchini
2 carrots
1 or 2 smooth skinned potatoes
2 dozen string beans
1 dozen mushrooms, cut in half
2 tablespoons of extra virgin olive oil (for basting)
1/2 teaspoon each of dried garlic powder, black
  peppercorns, dried oregano, basil and dill

PREPARATION

1 Slice Roma plum tomatoes in half. Wash and dry the radicchio leaves. Slice all of the remaining vegetables, except the beans and mushrooms, into one quarter inch pieces, lengthwise. Then cut the carrots into smaller lengths, about one eighth inch thick.
2 Prepare a charcoal grill or use a stove top grill.
3 Lightly brush the vegetables with olive oil and place on the grill.
4 Make a seasoning mixture of one half teaspoon each of dried garlic powder, freshly ground black peppercorns, dried oregano, basil and dill. Sprinkle onto each side of the vegetables as they are being grilled. Add more as desired. Turn vegetables every five minutes or as needed. Brush on additional olive oil. Grill vegetables until they become lightly browned, scored, and soft.
5 Peel one or two cloves of garlic.
6 Charcoal grill, broil or toast eight slices of Italian bread.
7 While the slices are still hot, rub the garlic back and forth over the entire surface, including the crust.
8 Drizzle extra virgin olive oil onto each slice, or using a pastry brush, spread the olive oil onto each slice.
9 Using a grinder, sprinkle sea salt to taste on each slice.
10 Top each slice with one kind of grilled vegetable or a variety of them.

VARIATIONS

Use your own favorite spices or spice mixture; choose other vegetables to your liking.

ARTICHOKE, OLIVE AND TOMATO

Foods are a way of affirming and sharing one's cultural identity. . .

INGREDIENTS

8 half inch slices of Italian bread, 2 - 3 days old
2 cloves of garlic
1/3 - 1/2 cup of extra virgin olive oil
1 6 1/2 ounce jar of prepared artichoke hearts
6 kalamata olives
6 cerignola olives (green)
4 Roma plum tomatoes
2 tablespoons of fresh oregano leaves
1 tablespoon of extra virgin olive oil
black peppercorns

PREPARATION

1 Drain the liquid from the artichoke hearts and dice.
2 Slice away the kalamata and cerignola olive flesh from the pits and chop fine.
3 Quarter and then quarter again the Roma plum tomatoes.
4 Combine the artichokes, olives, Roma plum tomatoes, and fresh oregano. Add one tablespoon of extra virgin olive oil, freshly ground black peppercorns to taste, and toss lightly.
5 Peel one or two cloves of garlic.
6 Charcoal grill, broil or toast eight slices of Italian bread.
7 While the slices are still hot, rub the garlic back and forth over the entire surface, including the crust.
8 Drizzle extra virgin olive oil onto each slice, or using a pastry brush, spread the olive oil onto each slice. Sprinkle on sea salt to taste.
9 Spoon the artichoke, olive, and tomato mixture onto each slice.

VARIATIONS

Garnish with fresh basil.
Substitute dried oregano.
Add roasted and chopped pine nuts.
Sprinkle with Romano Pecorino cheese.
Substitute capers for cerignola olives.

SHREDDED CHICKEN

When what was left over topped my bruschetta,
I didn't know whether it was circumstance or invention
that resulted in exciting my palate.

INGREDIENTS

8 half inch thick slices of Italian bread, 2 - 3 days old
1 or 2 cloves of garlic
1/3 - 1/2 cup of extra virgin olive oil
2 large chicken breasts, deboned
1 carrot
1 small onion
2 stalks of celery

1/4 teaspoon of salt
4 or 5 springs of fresh parsley
1 tablespoon of extra virgin olive oil
sea salt and black peppercorns
1/4 cup of fresh basil, chopped
4 vine ripened Roma plum tomatoes
1/2 cup grated Pecorino Romano
   cheese

PREPARATION

1 Fill a four-quart pot two-thirds with water and bring to a boil. Turn heat down to medium and add two large chicken breasts and chopped carrot, onion, and celery. Season with one quarter teaspoon of salt and the springs of fresh parsley. Cook one hour.
2 Remove the chicken breasts to a large bowl. Allow to cool. Refrigerate the soup for future use.
3 Shred the chicken with a fork. Add one tablespoon of olive oil, sea salt and freshly ground black peppercorns to taste, and one quarter cup of fresh basil, chopped. Mix well.
4 Peel one or two cloves of garlic.
5 Charcoal grill, broil or toast eight slices of Italian bread.
6 While the slices are still hot, rub the garlic back and forth over the entire surface, including the crust.
7 Drizzle extra virgin olive oil onto each slice, or using a pastry brush, spread the olive oil onto each slice.
8 Cut thin slices of Roma plum tomatoes.
9 Spoon shredded chicken mixture onto toast. Layer very thin slices of Roma plum tomatoes on top and sprinkle with grated Pecorino Romano cheese.
10 Place on a large baking sheet and broil four inches from the heating element until the tomatoes become soft and the cheese melts.

VARIATIONS

Substitute a small turkey breast.
Use grated Mozzarella cheese.

FRIED GARLIC

*If we had to choose the food of the gods,
It would be garlic. . .*

INGREDIENTS

8 half inch thick slices of Italian bread, 2 - 3 days old
1/3 - 1/2 cup of extra virgin olive oil
10 large cloves of garlic
2 tablespoons of olive oil for frying
sea salt

PREPARATION

1 Peel ten large cloves of garlic (uncrushed).
2 Make a *soffritto*: fry the cloves of garlic (uncrushed) in two tablespoons of olive oil. Fry on low heat until the garlic becomes soft and only lightly browned, about five or six minutes.
3 Remove the garlic to a mortar with one tablespoon of the olive oil left over from frying.
4 Mash the garlic using the mortar and pestle until it becomes smooth and creamy. Then add the remaining olive oil from frying and blend it in.
5 Charcoal grill, broil or toast eight slices of Italian bread.
6 Drizzle extra virgin olive oil onto each slice, or using a pastry brush, spread the olive oil onto each slice.
7 Spread the garlic paste onto each slice.
8 Using a grinder, sprinkle sea salt to taste onto each slice.

VARIATIONS

Lightly sprinkle grated Pecorino Romano cheese on top (reduce salt).
Lightly sprinkle fresh or dried oregano on top.
Sprinkle freshly ground peppercorns, to taste.
Use regular salt.

EGGPLANT SPREAD

The major premise for preparing good foods. . .Keep it simple!

INGREDIENTS

8 half inch slices of Italian bread, 2 - 3 days old
8 cloves of garlic
1/3 - 1/2 cup of extra virgin olive oil
1 large eggplant
2 tablespoons of olive oil for frying
1 teaspoon of cumin powder
2 tablespoons of soy
2 teaspoons of tahini (sesame seed paste) mixed well
2/3 cup of pimiento

PROCEDURE

1 Cut the eggplant into quarters and then slice into half inch pieces.
2 Using a steamer or a colander and a large pot filled with four cups of water, steam the eggplant for fifteen minutes, or until soft.
3 Blanch the eggplant by immersing into a large pot of ice water. Drain well.
4 Put the eggplant into a colander. Press the bottom of a bowl onto it to remove excess liquid.
5 Make a *soffritto*: fry eight cloves of garlic (uncrushed) in two tablespoons of olive oil. Fry on low heat until the garlic becomes soft and only lightly browned, about five to six minutes.
6 Remove the garlic to a mortar with one tablespoon of the olive oil.
7 Mash the garlic using the mortar and pestle until it becomes smooth and creamy. Then add the remaining olive oil from the *soffritto* and blend it in.
8 Mix the cumin, soy, and tahini paste. Add the garlic mixture. Put in a food processor along with the eggplant and blend until smooth.
9 Prepare pimiento by draining well. Slice into small pieces, about one quarter inch.
10 Charcoal grill, broil or toast eight slices of Italian bread.
11 Drizzle extra virgin olive oil onto each slice, or using a pastry brush, spread the olive oil onto each slice.
12 Spoon generous amounts of the eggplant onto the toast and top with a sprinkling of pimiento.

VARIATIONS

Substitute diced vine ripened Roma plum tomatoes for pimiento.

SALMON AND TOMATO

Bread, garlic, olive oil. . . the Italian epicurean trinity. . .

INGREDIENTS

8 half inch slices of Italian bread, 2 - 3 days old
1 or 2 cloves of garlic
1/3 - 1/2 cup of extra virgin olive oil
1 seven and a half ounce can of red salmon
1 medium onion
3 vine ripened Roma plum tomatoes
1 tablespoon of extra virgin olive oil
sea salt and black peppercorns

PREPARATION

1 Open the can of salmon and drain off liquid. Put the salmon into a large bowl.
2 Shred the salmon with a fork.
3 Dice the onion, cube the Roma plum tomatoes, and add to the salmon.
4 Add one tablespoon of extra virgin olive oil.
5 Add salt and fresh ground peppercorns to taste.
6 Mix all ingredients well.
7 Peel one or two cloves of garlic.
8 Charcoal grill, broil or toast eight slices of Italian bread.
9 While the slices are still hot, rub the garlic back and forth over the entire surface, including the crust.
10 Drizzle extra virgin olive oil onto each slice, or using a pastry brush, spread the olive oil onto each slice.
11 Using a grinder, sprinkle sea salt to taste on each slice. (optional)
12 Spoon the salmon mixture onto each slice.

VARIATIONS

Substitute tuna.

FINALÉ

Although we read and follow a recipe consisting of the same words,
from the same page and from the same book, our result may differ.
What does this say about human invention, creativity, and discovery?

As I have noted in the introduction, preparing *bruschetta* should involve creativity, invention and art. Like a musical composition, my recipes have begun simply, evolving into a body that focuses on harmony and variation. Therefore, it should be no surprise that I should give *SIMPLY BRUSCHETTA—Garlic Toast the Italian Way*, a unique finalé—one that will provide a sense of closure to recipes that result in a simple, tasty and visually pleasing antipasto. Thus, as a conclusion, celebrate with a party or a dinner for friends, relatives, or those from your workplace or neighborhood.

First, cut in advance enough slices of Italian bread for *bruschetta* (at least two or three slices per guest). Then prepare a wide variety of toppings of your choice, arranged individually in small dishes or collectively on large platters. Also prepare bowls of peeled garlic cloves, extra virgin olive oil, fresh and dried herbs and spices, a variety of cheeses—sliced and grated, coarse sea salt and fresh ground black peppercorns.

Then let invention begin as your guests grill or toast bread, rub on the garlic, and drizzle extra virgin olive oil on top according to the *Traditional Bruschetta Con Aglio* recipe on page 27. Then they can prepare their own *bruschetta* by selecting toppings to satisfy their palates. Listen to the hum of joy and to the oh's and ah's that emanate from your guests. Interpret all of their musings. Like the dynamic trumpets, the sweet violins and the silence between the notes of Allesandro Stradella's *Sonata for Trumpet and String Orchestra*, your presentation and your guests' creations will be a concert to remember. In fact, play the CD for the occasion.

Buon appetito!
Vittorio Pellegrino

INDEX

A
anchovy, 32, 49, 76
anise, 34
artichoke, 53, 59, 87
arugula, 43, 84
asiago, 18, 66, 78
Asians, 19
asparagus, 69

B
bacon, 85
basil, 28, 36, 37, 45, 50, 59, 64,
        72, 75, 88
beans
        fava, 70
        lima, 79
        string, 86
breads, 20-21, 27-91
bread crumbs, 64, 66, 75, 78, 80
broccolini, 77
broccoli rabe (rapini), 30
bruschetta, 27-91
        definition, 11
        list of recipes, 25
        preparation
            applying garlic, 15
            applying olive oil, 15
            toasting, 15
        pronunciation, 11
traditional bruschetta
        con aglio, 11, 27
bruschetto, 11

C
capers, 44, 83
caponata, 83
cardoon, 75
carrot, 72, 74, 86, 88
celery, 62, 67, 72, 74, 83, 88
chestnut, 82
chicken, 62, 74, 88
        broth, 62
        liver, pâte', 62
cucumber, 58
cumin, 90
currants, 45

D
dandelions, 43, 56, 79
dill, 85

E
egg, 63, 64, 66, 75, 80
eggplant, 54, 57, 67, 83, 86, 90
endive, 43

F
fava, 70
fettunata, 11
finocchio, 78
fontina, 18
fontinella, 18, 41
Food of Italy, 11

G
garlic, 23, 27-91
        fried, 89
        roasted, 41
        soffritto, 56, 77, 84, 89, 90
        softneck, 23
gorgonzola, 18, 19, 33

H
ham hock, 79

I
Italian
        breads, 20-21, 27-91
        cheese, 18
            cardinal rules for, 19
        sausage, 39
Italy, Food of, 11
Italy, map of, 7

L
lemon, 73
lima beans, 79
liver, chicken, 62

M
marinara, 35, 64
marrow, bone, 72
measurements, 17
melon, cantaloupe, 42
mozzarella, 18, 34, 37, 40, 57, 59,
        60, 80
mushroom, portabella, 40

N
Niagara Falls
        DiCamillo Bakery, 20

O
olive oil, 22, 27-91
        extra virgin, 22, 27-91
        virgin, 22
        light, 22
        pure, 22
        pomace, 22
olives, 52, 61, 83, 87, 88
onion, 31, 32, 33, 39, 40, 55, 62,
        67, 70, 71, 72, 74, 79, 83,
        86, 88, 91
orange, 49
oregano, 31, 35, 47, 58, 61, 67,
        68, 80, 87

P
pancetta, 56, 70
parmigiano-reggiano, 18, 28, 54
parsley, 50, 52, 62, 64, 66, 67, 72,
74, 75, 88
pecorino-Romano, 18, 19, 35, 36,
53, 61, 64, 74, 75, 88
peppercorns, 65
peppers
        bell, 29, 39, 67, 71, 86

peppers
        pimiento, 78, 90
        red chili, 38, 55
        roasted, 46, 53, 66
        sweet caribe banana, 51
pesto, 28
pine nuts, 45, 83, 85
polenta, 64
potato, 86
proportions, 17
prosciutto, 42
provolone, 18, 19

R
radicchio, 86
ricotta, 18, 19, 52
romaine, 43
Root, Waverly, 11
rosemary, 55

S
salmon, 44, 91
sardines, 73
scallions, 76
schiena d'asino, 11
shallots, 60
soffritto, 56, 77, 84, 89, 90
soup stock, 74
soy, 90
spinach, 63
squash, butternut, 85
Stradella, Allesandro
        Sonata for Trumpet
        and String Orchestra, 92
substitutions, 24
sugar, 83

T
tahini, 90
tomato
        green, 68
        Roma plum, 37, 45, 47, 50, 53,
        60, 76, 81, 83, 84, 87, 88, 91
        sun-dried, 86
        whole, canned, 31

V
variations, 24
        in recipes, 27-91
vinegar
        balsamic, 37, 43, 58, 60, 83
        cider, 67, 73

Z
zucchini, 48, 86

ABOUT THE AUTHOR

Vittorio C. Pellegrino has enjoyed cooking for as long as he can remember. He began preparing simple foods at an early age. His experience as a Boy Scout gave him additional opportunities to cook over campfires and hot kitchen stoves, sometimes for large groups. During his high school and early college years, he worked as a short order cook, a bartender, a busboy, a soda jerk, and a cook at a private boy's camp in Canada. When he married Wallette Garcia of Maui and they began their family, he continued preparing Italian and American foods as part of his love for cooking as well as to share family responsibilities. After moving to Hawai'i in 1967, he became interested in the many multi-ethnic foods there, including Hawaiian dishes. Then after his travels to Asia, he began experimenting and perfecting dishes from India, China, Japan and Korea.

But underlying all of his interests in multi-ethnic foods, nothing is more deeply rooted in him than cooking Italian dishes. Several years ago he began experimenting with a variety of toppings for *bruschetta con aglio*. From his culinary creativity came a few extra pounds, which he has now taken off, and a passion for preparing and sharing his recipes. And sharing is what has led to the publication of *SIMPLY BRUSCHETTA—Garlic Toast the Italian Way*. He has taught and continues to teach many classes on pasta making, sauces, and *bruschetta* for Maui Community College, Department of Continuing Education and for community groups.

Pellegrino, Professor Emeritus, taught writing and literature at Maui Community College for twenty-eight years, and served eight years as chairperson of the Language Arts Division. Recently he taught upper division classes in advanced writing and American literature for the University of Hawai'i, Maui Outreach.

Recognized as a statewide leader in the field of writing, Pellegrino was the first recipient of the *Excellence in English Teaching Award* presented by the Hawai'i affiliate of the National Council of Teachers of English. He also received the *Excellence in Teaching English Award* from the Hawai'i Branch of the English-Speaking Union of the United States. Pellegrino has served on the editorial board of Makali'i, The Journal of the University of Hawai'i Community Colleges, and has edited for publication many manuscripts.

Pellegrino's books have guided writers for nearly two decades. *A Writer's Guide to Transitional Words and Expressions* was first published in 1987 and is now in its sixth printing. *A Writer's Guide to Using Eight Methods of Transition*, published in 1993, serves as a complementary text to his popular transitional words book. In 1984, Pellegrino published two writing books designed for use in Hawai'i schools, *You Can Write! Practical Writing Skills for Hawai'i*, and *You Can Write Workbook*. His newest writing book, published in 2001, is titled *How to Write Powerful Paragraphs 30 Ways*.

Pellegrino's writings are not limited to the world of English. He has written two reflective books, *Maui Art Thoughts—Expressions and Visions*, and *A Slip of Bamboo—A Collection of Haiku from Maui*. Within the next two years he plans to publish his ninth book, a novel, now in manuscript form.

During his teaching career, Pellegrino developed a unique interdisciplinary Eastern world literature course emphasizing the writings of India, China, and Japan. This course complemented Pellegrino's Western world literature course emphasizing Europe, Africa, and Russia.

In addition to his own writing, Pellegrino has edited and published sixteen books for other authors from Hawai'i and the Mainland. He has also taught many self-publishing seminars for Maui Community College, Department of Continuing Education.

Pellegrino received B.S. and M.S. degrees from the State University of New York, College at Buffalo. He has studied and traveled extensively in Japan and China, and in 1984 he was a Fulbright Scholar in India. He is married to Wallette Garcia of Wailuku, Maui. They have three children, Shelley, Angela, and Hōkūao.

BOOKS BY PELLEGRINO

Order any number of copies of one title or mixed titles. All titles listed below are also available at **special discounts for bulk purchases,** such as for sales promotions, conventions, premiums, fundraisers (schools, home schools, libraries, churches, non-profit and for-profit organizations, etc...), and for reselling. Phone or Fax our order hotline **TOLL FREE: 1-800-403-3472,** write us at the address below, contact us via e-mail at **books@maui.net** or check our websites at **booksmaui.com** OR **mauiarthoughts.com**

■ *SIMPLY BRUSCHETTA—Garlic Toast the Italian Way*
    Pellegrino, Vittorio C. © 2001, ISBN 0-945045-06-9, hard cover, $18.95
■ *How to Write Powerful Paragraphs 30 Ways*
    Pellegrino, Victor C. © 2001, ISBN 0-945045-05-0, soft cover, $15.95
■ *A Writer's Guide to Transitional Words and Expressions*
    Pellegrino, Victor C. © 1989, 6th Printing 1999, ISBN 0-945045-02-6, soft cover, $9.95
■ *A Slip of Bamboo—A Collection of Haiku from Maui*
    Pellegrino, Victor C. © 1996, ISBN 0-945045-04-2, soft cover, $7.95
■ *A Writer's Guide to Using 8 Methods of Transition*
    Pellegrino, Victor C. © 1993, ISBN 0-945045-03-4, soft cover, $5.95
■ *Maui arThoughts—Expressions and Visions*
    Pellegrino, Victor C. © 1988, ISBN 0-945045-01-8, soft cover, $9.95
■ *You Can Write! Practical Writing Skills for Hawai'i*
    Pellegrino, Victor C. © 1982, ISBN 0-935848-04-5 (out of print)
■ *You Can Write Workbook*
    Pellegrino, Victor C. © 1983, ISBN 0-935848-28-2 (out of print)

- Use the **ORDER FORM** on the next page
- When ordering by mail, send a check, money order, or purchase order.
- Include S&H.
- Payment should be made to Maui arThoughts Company (US funds).
- Include bill to and ship to addresses if different.
- For phone, fax or e-mail orders, shipments will include an invoice.
- Special discounts available to bookstores, educational institutions, & libraries.
- Inquire about special quantity order discounts.
- Prices and S&H costs are subject to change without notice.

Maui
arThoughts
Company

... the creative publisher with books that work ...

P.O. Box 967
Wailuku, HI, USA 96793-0967
Phone/Fax: 808-244-0156
Phone/Fax Toll Free (orders): 800-403-3472
email: books@maui.net
booksmaui.com OR mauiarthoughts.com

ORDER FORM

Mail. . . Phone. . . Fax. . . E-mail. . . or .Com

■MAIL ORDERS TO: Maui arThoughts Company
■P.O. Box 967, Wailuku, HI, USA 96793-0967
■PHONE-FAX FOR INFORMATION/INQUIRIES: 808-244-0156
■PHONE-FAX ORDERS TOLL FREE: 800-403-3472
■E-MAIL ORDERS TO: books@maui.net
■WEBSITES: booksmaui.com OR mauiarthoughts.com

■**PLEASE SEND ME:**

☐ **SIMPLY BRUSCHETTA—Garlic Toast the Italian Way** @ $18.95 per copy	$
☐ **How To Write Powerful Paragraphs 30 Ways** @ $15.95 per copy	$
☐ **A Slip of Bamboo—A Collection of Haiku from Maui** @ $7.95 per copy	$
☐ **A Writer's Guide to Transitional Words and Expressions** @ $9.95 per copy	$
☐ **Writer's Guide to Using Eight Methods of Transition** @ $5.95 per copy	$
☐ **Maui Art Thoughts—Expressions and Visions** @ $9.95 per copy	$

SUBTOTAL	$
DISCOUNTS (Include Purchase Order)	
• Retail Bookstores, less 40%	$ -
• College/University Bookstores, less 20%	$ -
• Schools & Libraries, less 10%	$ -
TAXES	
• HI Residents (Include .04166 Sales Tax)	$+
• HI Bkstrs., Schools & Libraries (Include .005 Whsl. Tax)	$+
SHIPPING	
• 1st Class S&H *(See Below OR if you wish, leave blank. We will compute S&H & bill you)*	$+
TOTAL AMOUNT DUE	$

■**BILL TO:**
Name _____

Address _____

City _____ State_____ Zip_____

Phone _____ Fax _____

■**SHIP TO:**
Name _____

Address _____

City _____ State_____ Zip _____

E-mail _____

■**PAYMENT:**
☐ Check/Money Order
☐ Purchase Order Number
☐ (Attach P.O. to Order Form)
☐ Bill Me

1st Class/Priority Air Mail ✈ U.S. Postal Service (S&H)		
# of Copies	Hawai'i	All Other States
1	3.50	3.50
2-3	4.50	5.50
4-5	5.50	7.50
6-15	7.00	9.00
16-20	7.75	10.50
21-28	8.75	13.75
29-37	9.25	16.00
38-47	10.50	18.50
48-57	11.25	21.50
58-66	13.00	24.50
67-75	14.00	26.00
76 or more*		

— *Additional Shipping and Handling Information* —
♦ Use the chart to the left for all books EXCEPT *Simply Bruschetta*. For *Simply Bruschetta*, HI residents add $3.50 for 1 book & $2.00 for ea. add'l. book up to 10 copies. For all other states, add $3.50 for 1 book & $3.50 for each add'l. book up to 10 copies. If you order a mix of titles or more than 10 copies of *Simply Bruschetta*, we can compute S&H and bill you. ♦ The chart at the left is limited to 76 or fewer copies of any title except *Simply Bruschetta* (see above). We will bill you for USPS S&H costs. ♦ We can also bill & ship via UPS. ♦ We can also ship via USPS Fourth Class Book Rate, but allow a minimum of 6-8 weeks for delivery. ♦ We can fulfill special arrangements & requests for orders from foreign countries & bill you for S&H costs. ♦ Include bill to and ship to addresses if different. ♦ S&H charges are subject to change based upon U.S. Postal Service and UPS rate increases.

• **NOTE:** Book prices and S&H costs are subject to change without notice.